Up & Running with
PC Tools Deluxe 6

Up & Running with PC Tools™ Deluxe 6

Thomas Holste

San Francisco • Paris • Düsseldorf • Soest

Acquisitions Editor: Dianne King
Translator: John Cantrell, Tristan Translations
Revisor: Richard Schwartz
Editor: David Clark
Technical Editor: Dan Tauber
Word Processor: Deborah Maizels
Book Designer: Elke Hermanowski
Screen Graphics: Delia Brown
Desktop Publishing Operator: Deborah Maizels
Proofreaders: Edith Rex and Rhonda Holmes
Indexer: Ted Laux
Cover Designer: Kelly Archer

PC Tools is a trademark of Central Point Software, Inc.
SYBEX is a registered trademark of SYBEX, Inc.

TRADEMARKS: SYBEX has attempted throughout this book to distinguish proprietary trademarks from descriptive terms by following the capitalization style used by the manufacturer.

SYBEX is not affiliated with any manufacturer.

Every effort has been made to supply complete and accurate information. However, SYBEX assumes no responsibility for its use, nor for any infringement of the intellectual property rights of third parties which would result from such use.

Library of Congress Card Number: 90-70368
ISBN: 0-89588-678-2

Manufactured in the United States of America
10 9 8 7 6 5 4 3 2 1

Up & Running

Let's say that you are comfortable with your PC. You know the basic functions of word processing, spreadsheets, and database management. In short, you are a committed and eager PC user who would like to gain familiarity with several popular programs as quickly as possible. The Up & Running series of books from SYBEX has been developed for you.

Who this book is for

This clearly structured guide shows you in 20 steps what the product can do, how you make it work, and how soon you can achieve practical results.

What this book provides

Your Up & Running book thus satisfies two needs: It describes the program's capabilities, and it lets you quickly get acquainted with the program's operation. This provides valuable help for a purchase decision. You also receive a 20-step basic course that provides a solid foundation in the program—even if you're a beginner with scant prior knowledge.

The benefits are plain to see. First, you will invest in software that meets your needs because, thanks to the appropriate Up & Running book, you will know the program's features and limitations. Second, once you purchase the product, you can skip the instruction manual and learn the basics of the program by following the 20 steps.

We have structured the Up & Running books so that the busy user spends little time studying documentation and the beginner is not burdened with unnecessary text.

Structure of the book

A clock shows your work time for each step. This indicates how much time you can expect to spend on each step with your computer.

Clock

Naturally, you'll need much less time if you only read through the steps rather than carrying them out at your computer. You can also save some time by scanning the short notes in the margins to find the most important sections within a step.

Three symbols are used to highlight points of special note. These symbols and their meanings are shown below:

Symbols

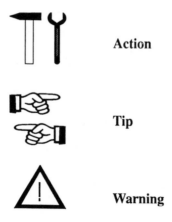

Action

Tip

Warning

An Up & Running book cannot, of course, replace a book or manual containing advanced applications. However, you will get the information needed to put the program to practical use and to learn its basic functions.

Contents

The first step always covers software installation in relation to hardware requirements. You'll learn whether the program can operate with your available hardware. Various methods for starting the program are also explained.

The second step introduces the program's user interface.

The remaining 18 steps demonstrate basic functions, using examples or short descriptions. You also learn about various facilities for printing data, displaying it on the screen, and importing and exporting it. The last steps cover special program features, such as a built-in macro language, additional editing facilities, or additional programs provided by third parties.

Steps 3–20

An Up & Running book will save you time and money.

SYBEX is very interested in your reaction to the Up & Running series. Your opinions and suggestions will help all of our readers, including yourself.

Preface

Personal computers have become virtually indispensable as business machines and entertainment centers, yet to the majority of users these machines still possess a mystique. The computer, while running a demo program or game, seems friendly enough until you attempt to use the commands in its operating system. MS-DOS and PC-DOS provide powerful functions for running and maintaining files on personal computers. However, DOS is not known for its user-friendliness.

There should be a way to make the computer do what you want it to without having to memorize cryptic DOS commands. PC Tools Deluxe Version 6 provides a fast and easy way to manage your computer. It contains the most commonly used DOS functions, while adding its own powerful array of utilities. It even provides a Desktop manager and a fast backup program.

The twenty steps in this book will lead you through the most important functions of PC Tools Deluxe Version 6. These steps will give you a firm foundation upon which to build while becoming acquainted with the package and its many features.

Richard W. Schwartz
March 9, 1990

Table of Contents

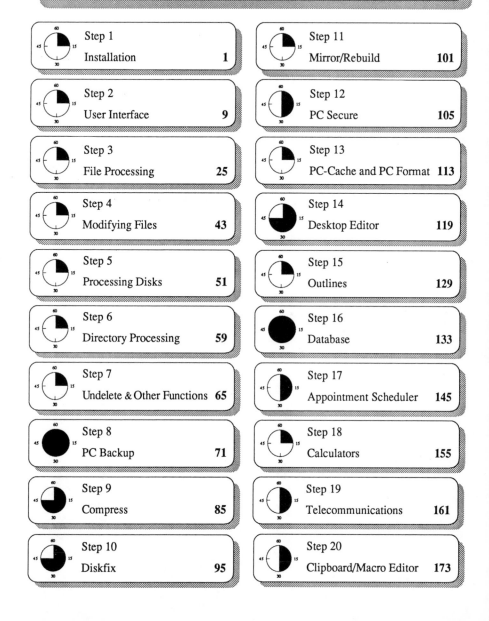

Step 1

Installation

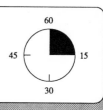

Before you can work with PC Tools Deluxe, you must install the program on your computer. This first step shows you the individual components that make up the software package and gives you information that will permit you to install the program according to your needs.

Contents

Overview of the New Version

The current version of PC Tools Deluxe (version 6.0) consists of several component programs that can be started either from a common user interface or individually from the DOS prompt. The main component programs are

Overview

PC Shell	a user interface/DOS shell
PC Backup	a backup program for your hard disk
Mirror/Rebuild	restores inadvertently formatted disks
PC-Cache	accelerates disk access by storing frequently used information in memory
Compress	optimizes the hard disk by reorganizing files
Diskfix	fixes common problems associated with hard drives and floppies
PC Format	replaces the DOS FORMAT command
PC Secure	secures files with a password
Desktop	a desktop manager

The Desktop program includes a word processing program, a database program that can handle dBASE III and dBASE IV files, and a powerful appointment scheduler. Desktop also contains a telecommunications program and other practical utilities.

PC Tools Deluxe also comes with a few smaller programs. These will be described in the appropriate context.

Hardware Prerequisites

PC Tools Deluxe runs on all IBM PC, XT, AT, and compatible computers. You must have at least 512K of RAM and DOS version 3.0 or later. DOS version 3.2 or later is recommended. If you plan to install any of the component programs to be memory-resident (there are definite advantages to this), it is recommended that you have at least 640K of RAM. Athough you can use parts of the program with one floppy disk drive, you can only make full use of the program with a hard disk. You may use all popular printers. The program also supports all video adapters. PC Tools Deluxe can take advantage of an EMS memory board, which improves the speed of the programs.

Making Backup Copies

First, you should make copies of your original floppy disks and use these copies to install the program. If you have only one floppy disk drive, enter the following command:

        DISKCOPY A: A: <Return>

Should your computer have two floppy disk drives, use this command:

        DISKCOPY A: B: <Return>

In either case, DISKCOPY will then guide you through the backup procedure, telling you when to switch disks and so on.

From this point on, you should always use the copies rather than the originals, in order to protect the original floppy disks from damage.

Installation

PC Tools Deluxe has an installation program that creates a directory on the hard disk and copies all the necessary files to that directory. Insert the first floppy disk into drive A and enter the following commands:

    A: <Return>

and then type

    PCSETUP <Return>

A dialog box will appear, asking you to specify whether the program is to be installed on a single PC or on a network server. Choose whichever option is applicable. (You are also given an opportunity to change the configuration of a previous installation. This choice would not be applicable to a first installation; if you decide to reconfigure at a later time, selecting this choice will bring up the appropriate instructions.) The next window (shown in Figure 1.1) instructs you to select the program components to be installed. The first choice includes PC Shell. This window also displays the hard disk space requirements for each choice.

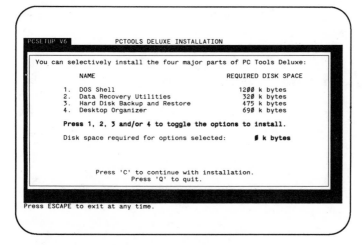

Figure 1.1: Choosing the main program groups

Using PC Tools Deluxe without a Hard Disk

The program makes no provision for installation without a hard disk. If you want to use any component programs without a hard disk, you must start these programs from the appropriate floppy disk(s). Note that without a hard disk most of the component programs operate only to a limited degree, if at all.

The installation program will lead you through the process of copying the selected programs from the appropriate floppy disks onto the hard disk. It will also update the DOS AUTOEXEC.BAT file to include the PC Tools Deluxe directory. This allows you access to the selected programs from any DOS prompt. In addition, the program renames the DOS FORMAT command to FORMAT! and replaces it with the PC Tools Deluxe program named PC Format. This program formats disks in such a way that PC Rebuild can restore them if you format them inadvertently.

During installation, you may select from various options. For instance, you may install PC Shell and Desktop to be memory-resident. Choose this option for PC Shell if you want it immediately available while in any other application. Desktop can be installed in a similar fashion. If you are planning to use Desktop applications, installing Desktop as a memory-resident program guarantees the fullest use of its many functions. PC Shell can also be installed as a DOS shell. In this mode it becomes the user interface, similar to the DOS 4.0 shell, and it will start automatically whenever you boot your computer.

Remember that installing programs as memory-resident can result in conflicts with other memory-resident programs. You may have to test the sequence in which you install memory-resident programs, because this can greatly affect operation. If you use SideKick, for instance, you must load it after PC Shell and Desktop.

Starting the Program

You can still start any of your programs from the DOS prompt by entering the program name, or you can start the programs from PC Shell (except when you have entered PC Shell from another program using a "hot key" combination).

To start PC Shell, enter the following:

```
C:\>PCSHELL <Return>
```

After you call the program, the user interface (which will be discussed in Step 2) appears. All functions from this point on are called from the user interface.

Start-Up Parameters

You can customize PC Tools programs somewhat by using start-up parameters when calling the various component programs. The parameters listed in Table 1.1 are the same for all programs. You will find other program-specific parameters discussed as appropriate elsewhere in this book.

Using parameters

Start-up parameters	Effect
/BW	Improved display on black-and-white monitors
/IM	Switches off the mouse pointer (for instance, if you have an older mouse, it might not work with all PC Tools Deluxe programs)

Table 1.1: Start-up parameters for PC Tools Deluxe programs.

Calling the Program When it Is Memory-Resident

If you did not opt for programs to be memory-resident during their installation with PC Setup, you can still install them in memory-resident mode by calling them and using the /R start-up parameter. Extended /R parameters can be used when calling PC Shell in order to allocate the amount of memory it occupies when it is inactive but still in memory-resident mode. These parameters are shown in Table 1.2. If you select a smaller number, you will have more space left free for other applications, but more time will be required to enter, exit, and operate the program. For most applications, it is recommended you choose the /RTINY parameter.

Start-up parameter	Main memory occupied
/RTINY, /R or /RT	10K
/RSMALL or /RS	88K
/RMEDIUM or /RM	120K
/RLARGE or /RL	225K

Table 1.2: Parameters for allocating PC Shell memory usage

For example, to load PC Shell with a main memory allocation of 120K on a system with a black-and-white monitor in memory-resident mode, enter the following command:

```
C:\> PCSHELL /BW /RM <Return>
```

Removing memory-resident programs

You can remove programs from memory by using the KILL program, but only if PC Shell and Desktop were the last programs to be loaded as memory-resident. Start the Kill program by entering the program name:

```
C:\> KILL <Return>
```

A screen message will report the completion of the removal of memory-resident programs.

Exiting the Programs

Stopping the program

All programs using the common user interface have a menu item to exit the program. However, it is easier to exit the program by pressing the Esc key or F3. After pressing the appropriate key, you must confirm that you wish to exit the program by pressing X. Exception: Desktop does not ask you to confirm that you wish to exit the program.

Mouse

You can operate all PC Tools Deluxe programs using a Microsoft-compatible mouse. In the following chapters, mouse operation will be described separately only when there are differences from the keyboard entries.

Step 2

User Interface

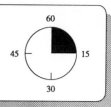

The user interface provides all input and output. It provides for easy use of the program and may itself be configured in several different ways. In this chapter, you will learn how to use the interface to select individual program functions and how to configure the interface to further simplify its use.

Contents

Screen Layout

All the PC Tools Deluxe programs have a uniform user interface that varies only slightly from one program to another. The differences will be described in the appropriate chapters. The user interface described below (and shown in Figure 2.1) is from the PC Shell program.

*User
interface*

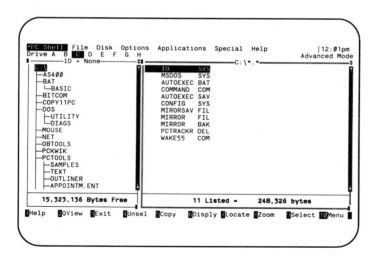

Figure 2.1: The user interface for PC Shell

The top line of the PC Shell screen contains various menus and the time display. The second line displays the available drives (with the current drive highlighted) and the user mode.

File and directory window

When you first call PC Shell, two windows cover most of the screen. The window on the left shows the directory structure and subdirectories of the selected drive, and the window on the right displays the files present in the current directory.

Status line

A status line is displayed below the two windows. This line provides information on the files in the current directory. Here you see how many files the directory contains and the amount of space used by each. This line also displays how much space is available on the current drive.

Command line

The line below the status line is the command line. It has two modes. The first mode functions as a DOS command line. You can enter DOS commands just as you would from any DOS prompt. The second mode is the Short Cut Keys line. It displays the most often used functions, which you may call simply by pressing the indicated key—you do not need to first select the desired function from the corresponding pull-down menu.

Message bar

The message bar follows the command line. Until you select a menu, the message bar displays the programmable function key assignments. All the function keys, except for F1, F3, and F10, are programmable by the user. However, the default function keys are used in this book. When you select a menu, the message bar changes to display a brief description of relevant functions.

Desktop User Interface

Desktop

The user interfaces of PC Shell and Desktop differ slightly. If you start Desktop, you will not see a file window, but rather a pull-down menu that enables you to select the various Desktop applications.

Other menus will appear as needed, depending on which application you select. Most of the Desktop applications appear in separate windows, and up to 15 windows may be open at one time. Generally these windows will overlap each other in the order that you call them; however, you can resize and reposition almost any window at any time so that several applications can be displayed on the screen at once (as shown in Figure 2.2).

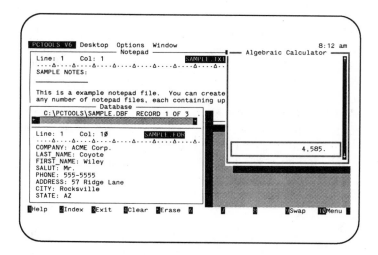

Figure 2.2: The Desktop user interface, showing several windows simultaneously

Menu Selection

You can select the menus for working with files or drives in several ways. You can press F10, then move the cursor to the name of the desired menu and press Return, or you can press the Alt key and simultaneously enter the first letter of the menu name. (In PC Shell, the first letter alone is sufficient. However, this does not work in some other programs.)

*Selecting
menu
items*

The menu that appears then allows you to select the various program functions. You select the functions shown in the menus in much the same way you selected the menu. You can move the cursor to the function you want and press Return, or you can enter the highlighted letter that appears in the name of the function you want. Mouse users select menu items by simply clicking on the desired item.

Dialog Boxes

*Confirming
commands*

To reduce the danger of possible errors, many program functions ask the user, by means of a dialog box, to confirm the action to be executed. For example, you must confirm any deletion of files. In these dialog boxes, the easiest way to select the appropriate response is by entering the relevant highlighted letter, or by simply pressing Return if the appropriate response itself is highlighted or outlined. For example, the letter *x* in the word Exit and the Exit box itself are highlighted in Figure 2.3. Use the Tab key to switch options or to jump from option to option.

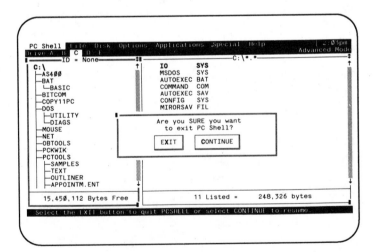

Figure 2.3: A dialog box asking for confirmation of an action

Other types of dialog boxes display groups of options, or items that require you to input information. In places where pressing a letter on the keyboard would simply serve to type that letter into an option box, selecting an option by pressing the appropriate highlighted letter entails pressing the Alt key in combination with the letter. Alternatives to this include using the mouse and clicking on the desired item, or, using the keyboard, pressing the Tab key to jump from group to group. (Pressing Shift and Tab simultaneously will reverse the direction the cursor moves.) Within a group, select the appropriate option by using the cursor keys. Enter the appropriate information and then press Return, or if no information is required simply press Return to select the item. Numbered options allow you to select more than one option at a time by simply typing the number(s) you want and then pressing Return.

Specifying the Drive

To change the current drive from PC Shell, press Ctrl together with the key corresponding to the letter of the drive. For example, select disk drive A by pressing Ctrl-A.

Selecting the drive

Specifying the User Mode

To make changes to the user level, pull down the Options menu and choose Setup Configuration. A pop-up menu will appear (as shown in Figure 2.4). Now select between Applications List Only, Beginner User mode, Intermediate User mode, or Advanced User mode by pressing the highlighted letter.

Changing the user level

The Application List Only mode lets you use PC Shell as an application menu. In this configuration, applications can be launched and files located. By pressing the F10 key you can access PC Shell as it was configured before selecting Application List Only. Beginner User mode offers simple DOS

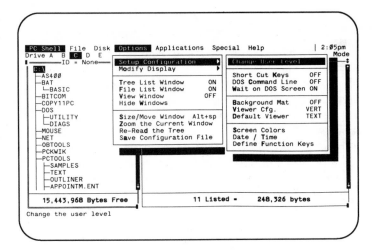

Figure 2.4: The Setup Configuration screen

commands. Intermediate User mode allows more complex use of DOS functions. Advanced User mode provides for maximum flexibility using PC Shell. The Short Cut Keys line is only available in Advanced mode. To turn on the Short Cut Keys line, pull down the Options menu and select the Setup Configuration pop-up menu. Choose the Short Cut Keys option. With the short cut keys on you will not have access to the DOS command line (see Figure 2.5). But for the sake of completeness it will be assumed the Short Cut Keys line is available.

Changing the Active Window

Selecting open windows

The active window is identified by a double-line border. Select files or directories within a file or directory window by moving the cursor bar by means of the cursor keys and then pressing Return, or, using the mouse, by clicking on the arrows at either end of the mouse scroll bar(s), as illustrated in Figure 2.6. Pressing a cursor key or clicking on a scroll arrow serves to move the cursor bar item by item (in some cases,

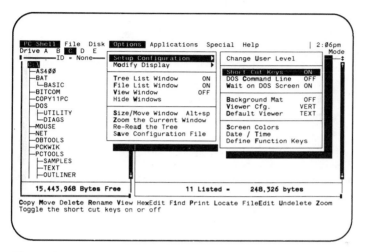

Figure 2.5: The Short Cut Keys line

character by character). Holding the mouse button when the mouse cursor is positioned on a scroll arrow speeds up the scrolling to a smoother, faster pace.

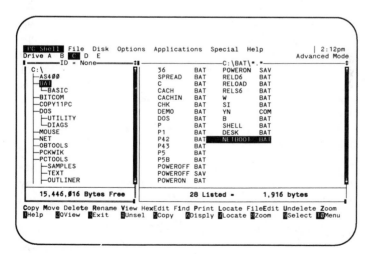

Figure 2.6: Mouse scroll bars

When a window is too small to display all of its contents, you may save time by using the scrolling features of the mouse scroll bar. Within the bar is a small box that indicates your relative position within the overall contents of the window; the closer it is to the top (in a vertical scroll bar) or to the left (in a horizontal scroll bar), the closer you are to the beginning of those contents. Dragging this box within the scroll bar can take you very quickly to an approximate location within a window's contents. This can be very helpful for finding pieces of a long note or document or for scanning the contents of a list that would take several screens to view completely.

To change the active window to another open window, press the Tab key as many times as it takes to reach the window you want. You can switch from one window to another with the mouse by simply clicking on the desired window—if you can see any of it. Note: Don't click on the upper left corner of any window if it contains a separate small box, because this is the window's *close box*. The dialog window in Figure 2.3, for example, has a close box.

Selecting open windows in Desktop

If you have more than one window open in Desktop and you wish to switch windows—from the database to the appointments scheduler, for example—select the Switch Active command in the Window menu or use the Swap command by pressing the F9 key. When more than two windows are open, a selection window will list each one. Select the one you want with the cursor keys and confirm your choice with the Return key or just press the highlighted letter corresponding to the selection.

If you can see any part of the window you want, the easiest way to switch windows is to use a mouse: simply click the mouse pointer anywhere in the desired window (except in the close box).

Displaying Two Drives or Directories

Pressing the Ins key instructs PC Shell to display two different drives or directories. The program divides the window area as shown in Figure 2.7. You may now work on two different drives or directories and their files.

Display-ing two drives

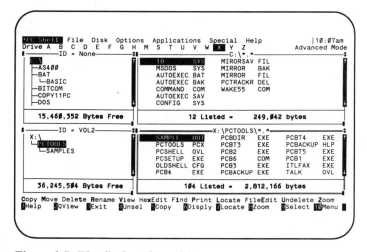

Figure 2.7: The display of two drives

You can switch from one pair of windows to another with F7. This function is particularly handy for copying files from one directory to another, because this feature immediately displays the files that are already present.

You can switch back to the normal display by pressing the Del key.

Changing the File Display

Pressing F6 displays a selection menu that can change the file display. This menu affords the option to display files with all information, such as the size, date, time, and attributes, or

Configur-ing the file display

only by name. You can also decide to have the files sorted by file name or extension.

Changing Screen Colors

If you have a color monitor and are not satisfied with the color display, you can change the colors.

In the PC Shell Options menu, select the Setup Configuration pop-up menu, then the Screen Colors function by entering the highlighted letter. Now select the colors for the file windows, status lines, and dialog boxes by entering the color number at each item. After making the selection, press the Tab key. Now you are asked to confirm the color selection. Pressing Return confirms the selection and ends the selection menu.

In Desktop, you change the color attributes in the Window menu. After selecting the Change Color function, a window control dialog box will appear. After selecting the colors you want, leave the dialog box by pressing the Esc key.

Moving Windows and Changing Window Size

Besides color, you can also specify window size and position. This is particularly important in the Desktop program, because you will probably be keeping several windows open at one time.

Configuring Windows in PC Shell

To change window size, press the Alt key and the spacebar simultaneously, or select the Size/Move Window command in the Options menu. In the submenu, select the Size option. You can then make all the appropriate changes by using the cursor keys, which act only on the bottom right corner of the window. Experimenting with this will give you the best idea of how the technique works. It is much easier to adjust the window size with a mouse. You can change a window by dragging the size box in the window's bottom right corner. First move the mouse pointer to that corner, then press either mouse button and hold it while you drag the size box to change the window size. Again, experimenting with this technique will give you the best idea of how the direction you move the mouse affects the sizing of the window.

In many cases, there is an even easier way to change the size of the active window—if all you want is to be able to see it better. When the command line at the bottom of the window displays the Zoom function, simply press Z to enlarge the active window. It will completely fill the work area of the screen. Pressing Z again restores the screen to its previous size. To move a window, press the Alt-Spacebar key combination, and the Window Control dialog box will appear. Choose Move and use the cursor keys to reposition the window. Using a mouse simplifies the process. You position the mouse cursor at the top border of the window, hold down the left mouse button, and drag the window to its new location.

Configuring Windows in Desktop

The functions for changing the windows in Desktop are found in the Window menu. Here again you have the option of changing the window size or moving windows. Configure the window with the cursor keys or with the mouse, as in PC Shell. Note that you cannot change the windows in all applications.

As in PC Shell, you can enlarge the active window in Desktop with the Zoom function, which, when it is available, is also found in the Window menu.

Closing Windows

You can close an active window by pressing Esc or F3.

To close a window with a mouse, click the mouse pointer on the close box in the top left corner.

Adding Application Programs

Application programs

During installation, PC Tools Deluxe automatically integrates some of the programs of PC Tools with certain other application programs, such as Word, Lotus 1-2-3, or dBASE, if they are on your hard disk. These programs can be called from the Applications menu of PC Shell. It is also possible to integrate other programs into the user interface. This is particularly useful when PC Shell is installed as a DOS shell. This way, you can start your word processor or database from PC Shell and return to it after leaving the application. Up to 20 programs can be integrated into PC Shell.

To integrate another program into PC Shell, first check to see which application programs have been added. Do this by selecting the Applications menu. The Applications menu will display the programs already integrated.

PC Shell will not stop you from adding the same application more than once, so be sure you check this window completely. Then press the F4 key to add a new application. The Applications menu will display a place holder where the new application will be inserted. You can reposition the place holder by pressing the up or down cursor keys. Press the Return key to confirm the position. You will see the window displayed in Figure 2.8. Now enter all the necessary information for starting the program:

Application: Enter the program name as you want
                        it to appear in the Applications menu.
                        You can instruct PC Shell to highlight

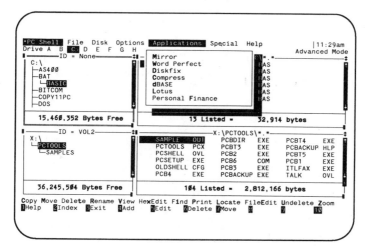

```
•PC Shell  File  Disk  Options  Applications  Special  Help        |11:29am
Drive A  B  C  D  E  F  G  H                         Advanced Mode
 ───────ID = None───────:│─┌─ Mirror ──────────────────┐N│*.*─────────
│C:\                     ▓│▓│ Word Perfect              │ │AS           ▓
│ ├─AS400               │ │ Diskfix                    │ │AS
│ ├─BAT                 │ │ Compress                   │ │AS
│ │ └─BASIC             │ │ dBASE                      │ │AS
│ ├─BITCOM              │ │ Lotus                      │ │AS
│ ├─COPY11PC            │ │ Personal Finance           │ │AS
│ └─DOS                 │ └────────────────────────────┘ │
 ─────────────────────────   ▄▄▄▄▄▄▄▄▄▄▄▄▄▄▄▄▄▄▄▄▄▄▄▄▄▄▄
  15,460,352 Bytes Free        13 Listed =    32,914 bytes

 ────────ID = VOL2────────:│────────────X:\PCTOOLS\*.*────────────────:
│X:\                     ▓│ ║ SAMPLE    OUT   PCBDIR    EXE   PCBT4    EXE  ║
│ └─PCTOOLS              │ ║ PCTOOLS   PCX   PCBT3     EXE   PCBACKUP HLP  ║
│   └─SAMPLES            │ ║ PCSHELL   OVL   PCB2      EXE   PCBT5    EXE  ║
                         │ ║ PCSETUP   EXE   PCB6      COM   PCB1     EXE  ║
                         │ ║ OLDSHELL  CFG   PCB3      EXE   ITLFAX   EXE  ║
                         │ ║ PCB4      EXE   PCBACKUP  EXE   TALK     OVL  ║
 ─────────────────────────
  36,245,504 Bytes Free        104 Listed =   2,812,166 bytes
Copy Move Delete Rename View HexEdit Find Print Locate FileEdit Undelete Zoom
1Help  2Index  3Exit   4Add    5Edit   6Delete 7Move   8      9       10
```

Figure 2.8: The Application Editor window

a letter within the name by entering a caret (^) character in front of the letter. This will enable you to start that program with a single key. For example, entering ^Edit allows you to start the program by simply pressing the E key.

Initial Directory: Enter the directory where the program is to look for files to process. This becomes the current DOS directory as soon as you run the application.

Execute Path: Enter the directory containing the executable program.

Run File Name: Enter the executable file name.

Run file Extension: Enter the executable file extension here.

Run parameter(s): Enter any desired start-up parameters here.

User prompt:

Prompts user to "Press any key or mouse button to continue" before executing the program. This is useful if a "key disk" is needed to run the program.

Keystrokes:

Allows a keystroke sequence to be passed to the program as keyboard input. The actual keystroke sequence may be entered, or, as in the case of a key represented by multiple letters, a key can be entered in angular brackets, for example, the Ctrl key. It is also possible to select commands from a list of key words. Just press the F8 key to view the list, use the up or down cursor keys to highlight the desired key word, and press the Return key.

File Specs:

Enter the files associated with the application.

Quick run this Application:

If you enter *yes*, PC Shell will not free up any of its memory before the application is run. It is not recommended that you use the Quick Run feature with large applications, because they might not have enough free conventional memory to run in.

Run with Selected File:

If you choose this option, files that you have selected in PC Shell are processed. This option is particularly suitable when you want a file name passed to the program as command line input.

Wait on Last
Application Screen:　　Decide whether you want to return from the program directly to PC Shell or to display an intermediate screen.

Exit to DOS when
Application ends:　　Enter *no* if you wish to be back to PC Shell after running the application.

Once you have entered the necessary information, confirm the entries by pressing the F4 key. If there are incorrect entries or you want to cancel an entry, select the F5 key to Edit or F3 key to exit.

Storing the Configuration

Once PC Shell is properly configured, select the Save Configuration function in the Options menu and store the settings. This ensures that PC Shell retains your configuration the next time the program is called.

Saving the settings

A few, but not all, programs in Desktop also provide for storing changes to the interface permanently. Select the Controls menu with the Alt-C combination. Then press F to start the Save Setup function.

Help

Pressing F1 in any progam displays a help dialog or message. The structure of the help system is context-sensitive; that is, the help text refers to the currently selected program function. An index that permits you to choose help messages for other functions is also available by pressing F2.

Help function

Changing Hotkeys

If you have other memory-resident programs that use the same key combinations as PC Tools for calling programs in memory-resident mode, you will have to change the PC Tools combinations.

Assign another key combination to PC Shell by calling it from the DOS prompt with a function key start-up switch /F*n*, where *n* specifies the number of a function key. From that point on you can call the program at any time by using the Ctrl key together with the selected function key. For example, the /F10 start-up switch makes Ctrl-F10 a hotkey.

In Desktop, choose the Utilities function in the main menu and select the Hotkeys Selection item in the following sub-menu. Press the desired key combination to select the new hotkey. For example, if you enter Alt-Home, you can use that same combination to call Desktop in memory-resident mode from then on.

Step 3

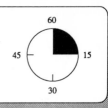

File Processing

The lack of simple file selection and processing facilities makes using DOS a headache. The inflexible operation of MS-DOS and PC-DOS is what makes this work complicated and troublesome. PC Shell's file selection and processing facilities provide a substantially faster and easier method.

This third step presents the various ways that PC Shell provides for file selection and processing. In this step you will learn how easy it is to copy and delete files in PC Shell and what file checking functions are available. PC Shell even provides for moving files, a function that MS-DOS and PC-DOS have not yet offered. In addition, this step describes the various options for printing text files. PC Tools Deluxe offers an additional tool for file handling between two computers. Laplink Quickconnect, developed by Traveling Software, comes with the package and allows the user to connect two computers together via a null-modem cable. The connection of two computers enables the user to transfer files from one hard drive to another directly. However, the cable is not provided. It can be purchased from Traveling Software at (206) 483-8088. This third step will show you how to easily copy files from one computer to another using the Laplink Quickconnect feature.

Selecting Individual Files

The greatest advantage of PC Shell is the option of selecting individual files for processing, independent of names and file extensions. Selecting individual files is particularly useful if you wish to copy or delete them in mass, regardless of names or file extensions. Proceed as follows:

Marking files

1. Tab to the directory window and select a directory with the cursor keys.

2. Switch to the file window with the Tab key. This window displays all the files in the selected directory.

3. Move within the file window with the cursor keys that control the cursor bar. Mark files with the Return key. A number corresponding to the sequence in which the files are selected indicates marking.

Selecting by Specifying the File Name or File Extension

Selecting file groups

To select larger groups of files, choose the File Select Filter function in the Modify Display pop-up menu under the Options menu or start this function by pressing the F9 key. Then enter a file name or a file extension. Both the "*" and "?" wildcards are available (see Figure 3.1). After finishing the selection, choose the desired file group by pressing the Alt-S key combination. The Alt-R combination allows you to make a new entry. Return to the main menu with Alt-C or Esc.

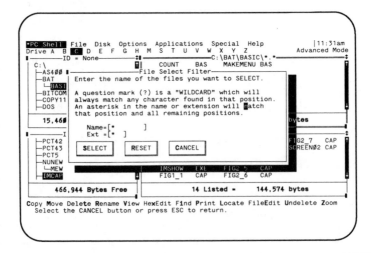

Figure 3.1: Selecting groups of files

Displaying Directory Information

All necessary information about the current directory is available in the first line beneath the directory display windows.

Directory infor- mation

The display specifies the number and size of the selected files, in addition to the number and total size of all files in the directory. This is particularly useful for copying files from the hard disk to floppy disks, because you can check at any time whether the floppy-disk capacity is exceeded. More specific information regarding the individual files is available with the More File Info function in the File menu (see Figure 3.2).

```
 PC Shell  File  Disk  Options  Applications  Special  Help          |11:31am
Drive A  B  C  D  E  F  G  H  M  S  T  U  V  W  X  Y  Z        Advanced Mode
         ID = None                              C:\BAT\BASIC\*.*
 C:\                                COUNT    BAS    MAKEMENU BAS
 ─AS400                      ──────More File Information──────
 ─BAT              File Name  : ORBIT
   ─BASIC          Extension  : BAS
 ─BITCOM           File Path  : C:\BAT\BASIC
 ─COPY11PC         File Attributes are : Normal
 ─DOS
  15,460,352       Last time file accessed  : 11/30/89 at 11:50am  ytes
                        The file length is   :        533 bytes
         ID = N     Total clusters occupied  :      1
 ─PCT42             Starting cluster number  :    974              IG2_7   CAP
 ─PCT43             Total files in Directory :     13              CREEN02 CAP
 ─PCT5
 ─NUNEW              EXIT
   ─MEW
 ─IMCAP
    466,944 Bytes Free              14 Listed -      144,574 bytes
Copy Move Delete Rename View HexEdit Find Print Locate FileEdit Undelete Zoom
  Select the EXIT button or press ESC to return.
```

Figure 3.2: Expanded file information

This function provides more detailed information, such as the last access date and the location of the file on the disk.

Cancelling the Selection

To cancel the selection of only one file out of a group of selected files, just use the cursor keys to position the cursor block over it, and press the Return key. To cancel all selections use the F4 key or the Reset Selected Files function from the Modify Display pop-up menu under the Options menu.

Restricting the Display

Selective display

Another function restricts the display area in the file window. Select the File List Filter function in the Modify Display pop-up menu under the Options menu or, as an alternative, press the F8 key. Enter file names or a file extension here the same way as when selecting file groups. Confirm the selection with the Alt-S key combination, or return to the main menu with Alt-C key combination.

The File Selection Window in Desktop

Desktop

In Desktop, files are selected for processing by using a file selection window(see Figure 3.3). The program displays files with the complete name in the window. The brackets enclosing names indicate directories. The program also displays the current path. You may proceed in either of two ways:

1. Specify the drive, path, and complete file name and file extension. The program loads the file, and it is ready for processing.

2. Specify only the file extension and press the Return key. If the file is not in the current directory, move the cursor bar to the drive letter and press the Return key again. Using the cursor bar, select the desired directory and confirm the selection with the Return key. Then select the desired file with the cursor bar and load it into the program by pressing the Return key once more. This method is somewhat cumbersome. It should be used only if you do not know where the desired file is or what it is called.

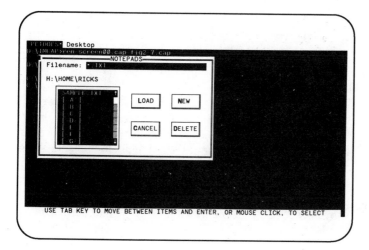

Figure 3.3: A file selection window

Copying Files

Copying files is the most common operating system function. In fact, many users tend to copy rather than create backups of their files because the DOS backup function is quite complicated. PC Shell makes copying files as easy as selecting them and pointing to where you want them.

Copying a file

To copy files, proceed as follows:

1. In the directory window, select the directory containing the files to be copied.

2. Tab to the file window and mark the files to be copied with the Return key.

3. If the Short Cut Keys line is available, press the C key or call the Copy File function in the File menu.

4. In the dialog window, choose the desired destination drive with the cursor keys and confirm the choice with

the Return key (see Figure 3.4). As an alternative, simply enter the drive letter.

5.   Using the cursor keys, choose the destination directory for copying, and then press the Return key.

The program now copies the selected files. For each file, there is a brief display on the monitor containing the source and destination drives and the path. After the program has completed copying, it returns automatically to the main menu.

If you have selected files that are already present in the destination directory, an additional dialog window appears as shown in Figure 3.5. You can specify further action in this window. The following commands are available if files are already present:

Replacing
Files

REPLACE ALL   Replaces all existing files in the
                             destination directory.

REPLACE FILE   Replaces only the current file.

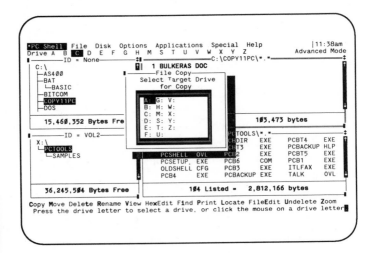

Figure 3.4: Selecting the drive

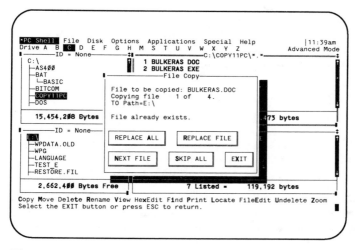

Figure 3.5: Error message if files already exist

NEXT FILE   Does not copy the file. The program proceeds with the next selected file.

SKIP ALL   Skips all files with name conflicts.

EXIT   Aborts and returns to the main menu.

Copying with Two File/Directory Windows

If you are working with the display of two directories or drives and want to copy files, the program always asks whether the second directory or drive will be used as the destination. If the answer is no, you must select a new destination directory with the cursor keys. This request also appears for other PC Shell functions when using double file/directory windows.

Two windows

Moving Files

An important extension to the operating system is the option of moving files from one directory to another. However, this

Moving files

is not limited to a single drive. For example, you can also move files from the hard disk to a floppy disk. This way, you save the time usually required to erase the files in the source directory. To move a group of files in a directory, proceed as follows:

1. Select the directory containing the files to be moved.

2. Mark the files.

3. Select the Move option in the Short Cut Keys line by pressing the M key or choose the Move File command in the File menu.

4. In the following dialog window, confirm that the selected files are to be erased from the source directory, using the Return key.

5. Using the cursor keys, specify the destination drive and then press the Return key.

6. Select the destination directory with the cursor keys and confirm your choice with the Return key.

For each file moved, a short message appears, confirming the operation and specifying the directory to which the program has moved the file. After moving all selected files, the program returns to the main menu.

Comparing Files

Comparing files

You can compare files using the Compare function in the File menu. This is useful when checking for errors in copying files from one place to another. It does not matter whether the files reside on different disks or in different directories. Compare files as follows:

1. Select the files to be compared with another file.

2. Call the Compare function in the File menu.

3. Specify the destination drive containing the second file.

4. In the following dialog window, decide whether files having the same name or different names are to be compared.

5. Select the directory containing the second file.

6. When comparing two files with the same name, a message appears specifying whether the files are identical or different. If you want to compare files having different names, specify the name of the second file after selecting the directory and press the Alt-C key combination. After the program has compared the files, a message will be displayed, specifying whether the files are identical or different.

7. Return to the main menu with the Return key.

Deleting Files

Using the Delete File feature found in the File menu is just as easy as copying or comparing files. Delete files as follows:

Deleting

1. Select the files to be deleted.

2. Choose the Delete option in the Short Cut Keys line by pressing the T key or call the Delete File function from the File menu.

3. In order to proceed, the following dialog window (see Figure 3.6) offers four different alternatives:

DELETE	Deletes only the displayed file.
NEXT FILE	Skips the current file.
DELETE ALL	Deletes all selected files.
CANCEL	Aborts the entire delete operation.

After deleting or skipping all the marked files, the program returns automatically to the main menu.

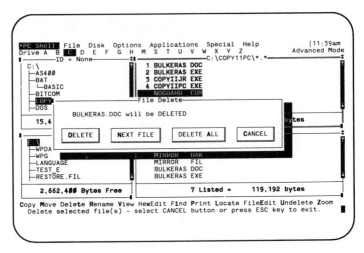

Figure 3.6: The Delete dialog window

Checking Files

Verifying a file

The Verify File function in the File menu verifies whether files are readable by checking every corresponding sector. Select the files to be verified and call Verify File. After verification has finished, a message regarding all the verified files will be displayed.

Printing Files

Printing

PC Shell has a wide variety of alternatives for printing files. The following steps are necessary to print a file:

1. Select one or more files. If several files are selected, they will be printed in the sequence they were marked.

2. Choose the Print option from the Short Cut Keys line by pressing the P key, or call Print File from the File menu.

3. In the dialog window, specify the printing modes by entering the highlighted letter. Three printing modes are available:

Print as a   Prints the file as a simple
standard test   ASCII test file.

Print file using   Gives additional options
PC Shell Print Options   for the printing layout.

Dump each sector   Prints the file sector by
in ASCII and HEX   sector in both hexadecimal
                                     code and ASCII.

4. Start printing by pressing the Return key.

Specifying Print Options

If you have selected the second printing mode, enter the printing options in the pop-up dialog box, as in Figure 3.7. Move the cursor bar to the desired option with the cursor

Defining printing

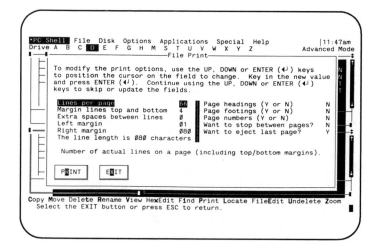

Figure 3.7: Printing options

keys. Then either enter a new value or start the option with the Y key. The following printing options are available:

Settings

> Lines per page
>
> Margin lines top and bottom
>
> Extra spaces between lines
>
> Left margin
>
> Right margin
>
> Page headings
>
> Page footings
>
> Page numbers
>
> Stop between pages
>
> Eject last page

Once the desired options are selected, start the Print command with the Tab key and confirm with the Return key. The program then prints the file according to the selected options.

Text Editor

Editor

PC Shell has a handy word processor option. It is not as powerful as the Desktop Notepads editor, but is quite useful for writing batch files or small text files.

Select the file to be edited with the cursor bar. Call the File Edit function in the File menu or from the Short Cut Keys line by pressing the E key. Specify in the dialog window whether you want to edit the file or create a new file as in Figure 3.8. Start the desired function with the Tab key and confirm the choice with the Return key. The program loads the file into the editor window, and you may now edit it.

The editor has its own editing commands. You will find the most important commands in the following table:

Editor
Commands

Key	Effect
Cursor keys	Move the cursor one position in the corresponding direction.
Home	Moves the cursor to the beginning of the line.
End	Moves the cursor to the end of the line.
Ctrl-Home	Moves the cursor to the beginning of the file.
Ctrl-End	Moves the cursor to the end of the file.
PgUp	Pages one screen backward.
PgDn	Pages one screen forward.

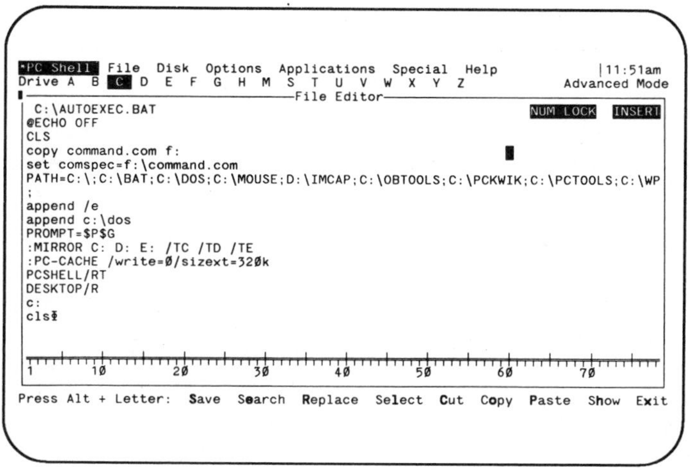

```
 PC Shell  File  Disk  Options  Applications  Special  Help          |11:51am
Drive A  B  C  D  E  F  G  H  M  S  T  U  V  W  X  Y  Z       Advanced Mode
                                  File Editor
 C:\AUTOEXEC.BAT                                             NUM LOCK   INSERT
@ECHO OFF
CLS
copy command.com f:                                      ▓
set comspec=f:\command.com
PATH=C:\;C:\BAT;C:\DOS;C:\MOUSE;D:\IMCAP;C:\OBTOOLS;C:\PCKWIK;C:\PCTOOLS;C:\WP
;
append /e
append c:\dos
PROMPT=$P$G
:MIRROR C: D: E: /TC /TD /TE
:PC-CACHE /write=0/sizext=320k
PCSHELL/RT
DESKTOP/R
c:
cls▓

 1       10        20        30        40        50        60        70
Press Alt + Letter:  Save  Search  Replace  Select  Cut  Copy  Paste  Show  Exit
```

Figure 3.8: The PC Shell editor

Finding and Replacing Text

Finding and replacing

To search for a character string, start the Find feature with the Alt-E key combination. Enter the character string and start the search with the Return key. Once the program has found the character string, return to editing mode with the Esc key or continue the search with the Return key.

To replace one character string with another, press the Alt-R key combination. Enter the character string and the alternate character string that is to replace the first. Otherwise, proceed exactly as with the Find function.

Marking a Text Block

Text blocks

To mark a text block, move the cursor to the beginning of the block and press the Alt-L key combination. Then mark the text block with the cursor keys. To abort the blocking of text, press the Alt-L key combination again.

Copying a Text Block

After marking a text block, press Alt-O and move the cursor to the point where you want to insert the text block. Press Alt-P to copy the text to the new location.

Moving a Text Block

Mark the text block and press Alt-C. Place the cursor at the position where the text is to be moved and press Alt-P.

Saving the File and Exiting the Editor

Saving the text

Save a file using Alt-S. Then leave the editor by pressing the Esc key or Alt-X.

Using Laplink Quickconnect

Installing Laplink

1. To operate the Laplink Quickconnect program, you must have the file LLS.EXE on the server or target computer. You can run it from the floppy drive or the hard disk. Type LLS at the DOS prompt and press the Return key. The default baud rate is 115200, and the default communication port is COM 1.

2. Next, you need to run the program LLQC on the source or client computer, which also needs PC Shell installed on it. Type LLQC at the DOS prompt and press the Return key. This is the TSR (memory resident) portion of the program. It too defaults to a baud rate of 115200 and COM port 1.

3. After running the program a screen appears indicating whether or not the program has been successfully installed. It will also show how the drives on the server will appear to PC Shell, as in Figure 3.9.

4. Now bring up PC Shell either resident, by pressing the hotkey combination, or non-resident, by typing PC Shell at the DOS prompt and pressing the Return key.

Using PC Shell to Access the Server

In PC Shell the server's drives will appear as the next available logical drives on the client computer. For example, if the server has one floppy and one hard drive and the client computer has floppy drives A and B and one hard drive C, then the server's floppy drive would be indicated as D and the hard drive as E on the client computer. If this sounds a little confusing, just think of the server's drives as additional drives available to the client computer. PC Shell will respond

```
C:\>llqc
              LapLink Quick Connect Version 6  successfully installed
              Copyright 1990 TRAVELING SOFTWARE, INC.

Configuration:
         Comport 1 in use at 115200 Baud

Local drive(s) mapped to Remote drive(s)

C:\>
```

Figure 3.9: Laplink Quickconnect configuration

to these additional drives like network drives. Many of the functions that are available to network users are available with Laplink Quickconnect. Conversely, the functions not available to network users are not available to Laplink users.

Transferring Files with Laplink

Transfer-ring files

1. Make sure the null modem cable is connected properly according to the instructions that come with it.

2. To copy files from the client to the server, call PC Shell and choose the client's source drive by pressing Ctrl-*N*, where *N* indicates the drive letter.

3. Select the file you wish to copy to the server by moving the cursor with the cursor keys, highlighting the file, and pressing the Return key.

4. Choose the Copy command from the File menu or use the Short Cut Keys line by pressing the C key.

5. In the dialog window, choose the desired destination drive with the cursor keys and press the Return key or simply enter the drive letter.

6. Using the cursor keys, select the destination subdirectory and press the Return key.

7. The main PC Shell screen will appear when the copying process is complete.

You will notice that the dialog windows are the same here as those described earlier in the copying files section. The only difference is that you are coping files to a remote computer.

The user can redefine the defaults that Laplink uses. The following is a list of parameters used by Laplink Quickconnect:

Parameter	*Definition*
/?	Displays a help screen listing all the parameters used by Laplink.
/U	Unloads the TSR portion (LLQC) from the client computer's memory.
/B:*nnn*	Sets the baud rate to *nnn*. The baud rate can be from 300 to 115200.
/C:*n*	Sets the communications port to COM port *n*. The default is COM 1.
/I:*n*	Sets the IRQ address to *n*. If you are using a serial card or internal modem with COM 3 or 4 support, you may need to change the IRQ for Laplink. Check your hardware manual for information on which IRQ your modem or serial port uses.

Redefining parameters

Make sure to define both the client and server computers with the same parameters.

Step 4

Modifying Files

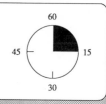

In addition to selecting and processing files, PC Shell provides many functions for changing files. These functions are available only in a rudimentary form, or not at all, as commands provided with MS-DOS or PC-DOS. The functions offered by PC Shell represent a substantial extension of the operating system commands.

This step shows how to search for character strings in files, how to edit binary and ASCII files, and how to change file names and attributes.

Contents

Renaming Files

Mark the file to be renamed and select the Rename File function in the File menu. If the Short Cut Keys line is available, press the R key. This is sufficient to start the function. After calling the function, specify the new name or the new file extension in the dialog window. Return to the main menu with the Return key.

Changing File Attributes

Changing file attributes is very easy with PC Shell. You can also change the date and time identification of files. To change file attributes, proceed as follows

File attributes

1. Select the directory containing the files that are to have their attributes changed. Then select the files.

2. Select the Attribute Change function in the File menu.

3. The Attribute window displays all the selected files in the directory, as seen in Figure 4.1. The file name, file extension, attributes, date, time, and file size are displayed.

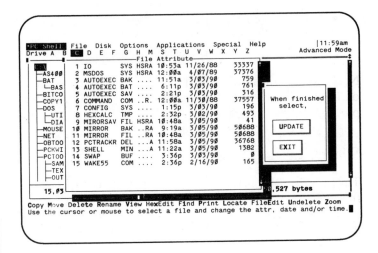

Figure 4.1: Attribute window

4. Change an attribute by moving the cursor to the attribute field and pressing the key assigned to the corresponding file attribute. Pressing the key again resets the file to its previous state. The following keys set attributes:

Key	Attribute
H	Sets the hidden attribute. The file is no longer displayed with the DOS command DIR and is inaccesible to some applications.
S	Sets the system attribute. The file is also no longer displayed.
R	Sets the read-only attribute. The file cannot be modified.
A	Sets the archive attribute.

5. To change the date and time, move the cursor to the appropriate field and overwrite the previous information.

6. Save the changes by pressing the U key. The program returns to the main menu. The new file attributes can now be displayed in the file window.

Never change the attributes of copy-protected program files or system files. Doing this is almost certain to create problems.

Searching for Characters in Files

The Text Search function on the File menu permits searching for character strings in files. Press S from the File menu to invoke this function, as seen in Figure 4.2. You can also call the Text Search function from the Short Cut Keys line by pressing the I key (the Short Cut key for this function is called Find). It makes no difference whether the search for characters is in text files or binary files.

Searching for characters

After you have called Text Search, enter the desired character string and start the search process with the Return key. The

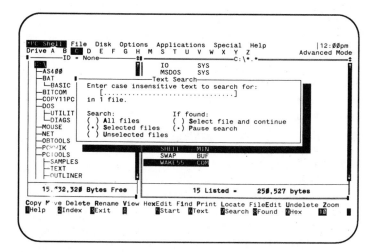

Figure 4.2: Searching for character strings

ASCII search is not case-sensitive and is limited to 32 characters. After entering the search term, additional search conditions may be specified.

To do so, press the Tab key and select from among these options: All files, Selected files, or Unselected files.

*Hexa-
decimal
characters*

To search for a string of hexadecimal characters rather than an ASCII string, switch to hexadecimal input mode with the F9 key. The hex search is case sensitive. If you enter an invalid hex value, PC Shell will alert you with a beep. Start the search process after entering the appropriate information.

Two processing alternatives are available once the program finds the search term. Use *Select file and continue* to mark the file and continue the search. Use *Pause search* to interrupt the search. The file may then be edited.

Hex Edit File Editor

*Editing
files*

In addition to the text editor, PC Shell has another editor that can be used to edit both text and binary files, as seen in Figure 4.3. However, it is not as well suited to text files as the text editor.

If you want to use the Hex editor, you should already have some basic knowledge of file editing. Using the editor, it is easy to patch, i.e., to change, program files. However, there is a risk of destroying important files. To edit a file, mark it with the cursor bar and press the X key. As an alternative, call the Hex Edit File function in the File menu.

The program displays binary files both in hexadecimal and in ASCII. The Alt-A key combination switches to the ASCII-only display. With the exception of text files, you can edit a file either in Hex mode or ASCII. To edit a text file you need

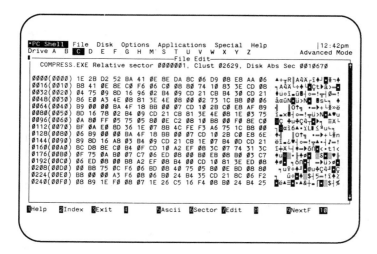

Figure 4.3: File editor—hexadecimal mode

to be in Hex mode. In hexadecimal mode, the screen shows one-half sector (256 bytes) at a time.

To select a different sector, press Alt-S. Enter the new sector number and return to the editor menu by pressing Alt-C.

Selecting a sector

Control the display of the selected file with the following keys:

Key	Effect
Home	Jumps to the beginning of the file.
End	Jumps to the end of the file.
PgUp	Scrolls backward one screen.
PgDn	Scrolls forward one screen.
F8	Toggles between HEX and ASCII editing.
Esc	Returns to the main menu.

Press Alt-E to edit the file. In addition to the listed keys, cursor keys can be used to move to any position within the

Editing mode

Editor window. Any desired changes can then be made. Once the cursor is properly positioned, simply type over the values to be changed.

Switch between the two editing modes with the F8 key. A file can be edited either in hexadecimal code or in ASCII code, as seen in Figure 4.4. Always make backup copies of your program files before editing. Remember that the editing function does not create a backup copy of the original file. If you decide not to make any changes, exit the editing mode by pressing the Esc key.

*Saving
the file*

Once the selected file is changed, return to the initial menu of the file editor with the F5 key. The editor saves the changed file, and it is available after leaving editor mode.

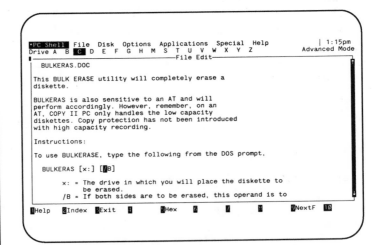

Figure 4.4: File editor—ASCII mode

Viewing Files

Any file can be viewed with the Quick File View function in the File menu, which you can invoke by pressing Q from the File menu or V from the Short Cut Keys line. The program displays binary files in the combined hexadecimal/ASCII mode, text files in the standard ASCII mode. As a special feature, Quick File View displays many file formats. The following list shows which files can be viewed in their native format:

Listing a file

Text files	Lotus 1-2-3 files (ver. 1a and 2.0)
Lotus Symphony files	Microsoft Works files
Microsoft Excel files	Borland Quattro files
Mosaic Twin files	Desktop Notepads files
XyWrite files	WordStar files
WordPerfect files	Microsoft Word files
DisplayWrite files	MultiMate files
Paradox files	dBase files (ver. 3 and 4)
Foxbase files	R:Base files
dBXL files	Clipper files
ARC files	Binary files
PCX files	PKZIP files
PAK files	LHARC files

Step 5

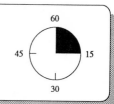

Processing Disks

Handling disks is just as easy as processing files. Many expanded functions simplify the utilization of floppy disks and hard disks.

This step shows not only how to copy, compare, and format floppy disks using PC Shell, but also how to verify and rename floppy disks and hard disks. This step also shows how to edit disks and explains character search functions.

Copying Floppy Disks

Copy floppy disks with the Copy Disk function found on the Disk menu. This is equivalent to the DOS DISKCOPY command.

After calling the function, proceed as follows:

1. Specify the source drive with the cursor keys. Next, press the Tab key and select the destination drive. Complete the selection with the Return key.

2. Insert the source floppy disk and press the Return key.

3. Insert the destination floppy disk and press the Return key again. (With some disk types, you may need to switch disks several times.) After finishing copying, the program returns to the main menu automatically.

Remember that copy-protected floppy disks cannot be duplicated with the Copy Disk function.

Comparing Floppy Disks

To analyze copies of floppy disks for possible copying errors, start the Compare Disk function in the Disk menu. As when copying floppy disks, first specify the source and destination drives and then insert the source and destination floppy disks, one after the other. If the program discovers errors when comparing the original and the copy, it displays these errors on the screen.

Formatting Floppy Disks

Formatting

To format a floppy disk, select the Format Data Disk function on the Disk menu. Proceed as follows:

1. Using the cursor keys, specify the floppy-disk drive to be used to format the floppy disk and confirm formatting with the Return key.

2. Insert a floppy disk into the selected drive, specify the type of formatting from Disk Installation menu shown in Figure 5.1 and press the Return key.

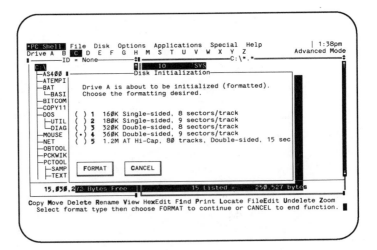

Figure 5.1: Specifying the format options

3. After formatting has finished, enter a volume name for the floppy disk. You can leave the disk with no name by simply pressing the Return key.

4. The floppy disk may also be made bootable. Space must first be reserved for the system files in order to do this. To reserve space on the disk, select the Bootable option using the Tab key. Then press the Return key. If the Skip command is selected, the program creates a normal floppy disk.

5. Upon completion, a status window displays the available space on the floppy disk and reports any damaged sectors. Return to the main menu with the X key or continue formatting with Return.

Creating System Floppy Disks

The Make System Disk function copies the system files and the command interpreter (COMMAND.COM) to a formatted floppy disk that has had space reserved on it for this purpose. Create a bootable floppy disk in the following manner:

System floppy disks

1. Select the Make System Disk function in the Disk menu.

2. Using the cursor keys, specify the drive and confirm the selection with the Return key. Insert a formatted floppy disk into the selected drive.

3. Confirm that you want the program to copy the files onto the floppy disk by pressing the Return key.

4. After the program has completed copying, it issues a message showing whether the file transfer was completed properly. Return to the main menu with the Return key.

Renaming a Floppy Disk/Hard Disk

Renaming

To change the volume name of a floppy disk or hard disk, select the Rename Volume function in the Disk menu. Enter the new name and confirm the name change with the Return key (see Figure 5.2).

This function can provide the hard disk with an additional protection because newer versions of DOS require specification of the volume name when deleting a hard disk partition.

Searching for Files

Searching

Even small hard disks often contain more than 1000 files. For this reason, searching for a specific file can be time-consuming. To find files quickly, together with any existing duplicates, proceed as follows:

1. Call the Locate File function in the File menu or press the L key from the Short Cut Keys line, and then press Return.

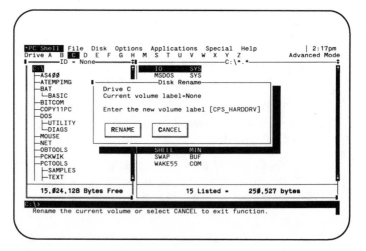

Figure 5.2: Renaming a hard disk

2. Enter the name and the file extension (see Figure 5.3). You can give multiple file specifications to include, each separated with a space, as well as specifications to ignore, prefixed with a minus sign. You then press Return.

3. Now you can enter text to search for in the files that meet the specifications. Enter the text and then press Return. If no text is entered, all the files that meet the file specifications will be listed. Otherwise only files that meet the file specifications *and* contain the text will be listed.

4. The program displays all files satisfying the search condition in a window. The program also specifies the directory containing each file.

Searching for Character Strings

The Disk menu provides a function to search for character strings. Here, the program does not restrict the search to one or more marked files but extends it to the entire disk.

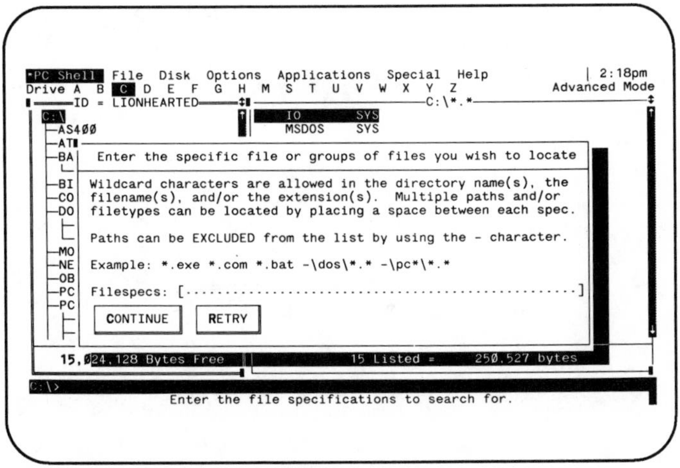

Searching for characters

Figure 5.3: Searching for files

Entire floppy disks or hard disks can be searched for character strings in this manner. This function is particularly useful
in searching for virus programs, for example, where part of
the binary code is known. Proceed as follows:

1. Call the Search Disk function in the Disk menu.

2. Enter the search term and press the Return key. To
   enter hexadecimal code, press the F9 key.

3. Once the program finds the character string or hexadecimal code, there are four main choices.

   Search   The program continues searching.

   Edit   Edit the character string found.

   Name   The program displays the name of the file
            containing the characters found.

   Exit   Return to the main menu with the Esc key.

Editing Data Media

Editing

The Disk menu provides an editor for binary files just as the
File menu does. The editing functions are identical, but a few
other commands are also available. To edit data on a floppy
disk or hard disk, proceed as follows:

1. Select the drive to edit.

2. Select the View/Edit Disk function in the Disk menu.

3. In the initial menu, select one of the commands for further processing. These commands are:

   Edit   Switch to editing mode.

   Name   Show the name of the file currently dis-
            played in hexadecimal and ASCII code.

   Sector   Specify the area of the disk to be displayed.

4. With the Sector command, you may select the following areas of the hard disk (as shown in Figure 5.4):

Boot Sector	The boot sector
First FAT Sector	The FAT (file allocation table)
First Root DIR Sector	The main directory
First DATA Sector	The first sector containing data
Change Cluster #	A specific cluster
Change Sector #	A specific sector

The danger of incorrect editing should also be discussed here. Use the editor only if you understand the implications of the changes. An altered boot sector can result in the computer no longer being able to boot from the hard disk. A FAT inadvertently damaged during editing will almost certainly result in

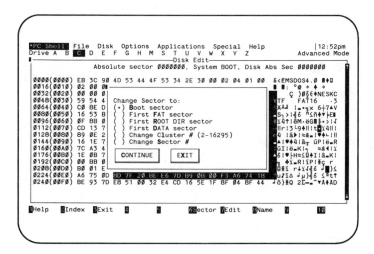

Figure 5.4: Selecting the sector

data loss. The editing commands are the same as those used in the file editor described in the previous step.

Verifying a Floppy or Hard Disk

Checking the disk

To examine your disk for damaged sectors, call the Verify Disk function in the Disk menu. This function checks each individual sector of the disk for readability. If it finds damaged sectors, it issues a message identifying the damaged areas.

Drive Information

The Disk Info function displays all relevant information for the selected drive. Information is displayed regarding the creation date, the free and the occupied disk space, and the capacities still available. In addition, the function provides information on the sector and cluster size and on damaged areas.

Parking the Hard Disk

Parking

Before switching off a computer, you should park the hard disk to protect it against damage from vibration or shock. (Note: Some hard disks park the heads automatically when the power is switched off. If you have a hard disk of this type, this step is unnecessary.) In order to secure the hard disk, call the Park Disk function in the Disk menu. This function parks the hard-disk head in the back area of the drive. Data that could be lost if the computer is jarred is not stored here. After parking the hard disk, switch the computer off. It does not matter that you have not exited PC Shell properly.

To continue working after parking the hard disk, return to the main menu with the C key.

Step 6

Directory Processing

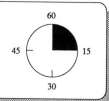

If you have ever tried to rename a directory under MS-DOS, you know just how inadequate the operating system commands are for processing directories. For example, renaming requires creating a new directory, copying all files, deleting the files in the old directory, and removing the old directory.

Changing directory names is much simpler with PC Shell. This step will show how to create, rename, delete, or move directories. Directories can even be hidden in an easy way.

An additional advantage of PC Shell is the ability to sort directories. Files may be displayed on the screen and printed, after being sorted according to numerous criteria.

The Directory Maint Menu

Select the Disk menu item in the PC Shell menu. Then press M to select the Directory Maint submenu for processing a directory. Within this menu, select the desired function by entering the letter shown in bold or a different color, or by making the selection with the cursor bar. (See Figure 6.1.)

If you are using PC Shell in memory-resident mode, remember not to change any directories containing files of the currently loaded program. This action will lead to complications because the program can no longer find important program files. Also, it is no longer possible to exit the application program safely without losing data.

Creating a New Directory

Start the Add a subdirectory function with the A key. First, specify the point in the directory window where you want to attach the new directory. To create a subdirectory one level

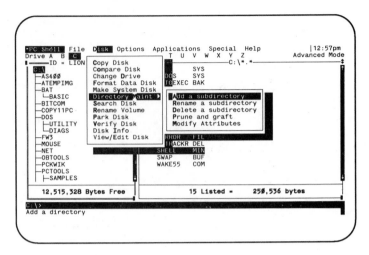

```
 •PC Shell  File  Disk  Options  Applications  Special  Help          |12:57pm
Drive A  B  C                     T  U  V  W  X  Y  Z         Advanced Mode
 ■──────ID = LION  Copy Disk                         ──C:\*.*──────────     ♣
 C:\                Compare Disk                  SYS
  ─AS4ØØ            Change Drive             DOS  SYS
  ─ATEMPIMG         Format Data Disk         TOEXEC BAK
  ─BAT              Make System Disk
   └─BASIC          Directory Maint ▶   Add a subdirectory
  ─BITCOM           Search Disk         Rename a subdirectory
  ─COPY11PC         Rename Volume       Delete a subdirectory
  ─DOS              Park Disk           Prune and graft
   ├─UTILITY        Verify Disk         Modify Attributes
   └─DIAGS          Disk Info
  ─FW3              View/Edit Disk     RROR   FIL
  ─MOUSE                                TRACKR DEL
  ─NET                            SHELL    MIN
  ─OBTOOLS                        SWAP     BUF
  ─PCKWIK                         WAKE55   COM
  ─PCTOOLS
   ├─SAMPLES

    12,515,328 Bytes Free                 15 Listed =    25Ø,536 bytes
 C:\>
 Add a directory
```

Figure 6.1: Directory Maint

below the main directory, move the cursor bar to the main directory and confirm the selection with the C key. You may also choose the Continue function with the Tab key and finish the selection with the Return key.

Next, specify the name of the new directory, as shown in Figure 6.2. An extension may also be added to the directory name. Create the new directory with the Alt-C key combination. The Alt-X combination aborts the program and returns to the main menu.

Renaming a Directory

New directory name

To give a directory a new name, select Rename a subdir in the Directory Maint submenu.

Using the cursor keys, move the cursor bar in the directory window to the directory you wish to rename. Confirm the choice by pressing C. Enter the new directory name by

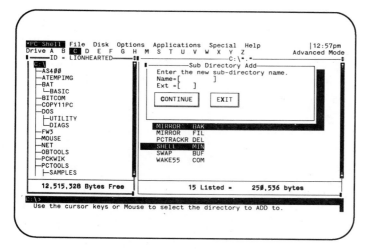

```
•PC Shell  File  Disk  Options  Applications  Special  Help        |12:57pm
Drive A  B  C  D  E  F  G  H  M  S  T  U  V  W  X  Y  Z         Advanced Mode
I———ID = LIONHEARTED———‡I ——————————————C:\*.*——————————————‡
 C:\                      I—————Sub Directory Add—————
  —AS400                    Enter the new sub-directory name.
  —ATEMPIMG                 Name=[         ]
  —BAT                      Ext =[    ]
   └BASIC
  —BITCOM                    CONTINUE        EXIT
  —COPY11PC
  —DOS
   ├UTILITY
   └DIAGS                  MIRROR   BAK
  —FW3                     MIRROR   FIL
  —MOUSE                   PCTRACKR DEL
  —NET                     SHELL    MIN
  —OBTOOLS                 SWAP     BUF
  —PCKWIK                  WAKE55   COM
  —PCTOOLS
   ├SAMPLES
  12,515,328 Bytes Free            15 Listed =    250,536 bytes
 C:\>
  Use the cursor keys or Mouse to select the directory to ADD to.
```

Figure 6.2: Entering the directory name and extension

simply overwriting the old designation. Confirm the name
change by pressing Alt-C.

Deleting a Directory

To delete a directory, select Delete a subdir by pressing D.
Move the cursor bar to the directory to be deleted and press
the C key. An additional prompt will be displayed before the
actual deletion takes place. This must be confirmed by pressing C again. To retain the directory, exit the program with the
X key. If files still exist in the directory, the program aborts
the deletion and displays an error message.

Deleting

Moving Directories

Another important function provided by PC Shell is the ability to move entire directories together with their files. To do
this, select the Prune and graft item in the Directory Maint
submenu by pressing P. A dialog box requests that you mark

Moving

the desired directory. Move the cursor bar to the directory and press C. After confirming the operation at an additional prompt, the program marks the selected directory with an angle bracket. Then select the directory you wish to graft it to by using the cursor keys. (See Figure 6.3.) Highlight the directory and press the Return key.

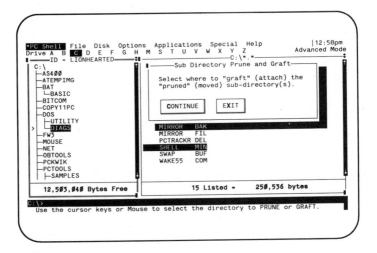

Figure 6.3: Specifying the destination directory

Next press the C key. Following a final prompt to confirm the operation with the C key, the program moves the directory. Sometimes, the directory window does not show the moved directory. This is because, upon loading, PC Shell reads the directory structure of the drive and stores it in a buffer. This is in order to change directories quickly. If after making a change you do not see it reflected in the directory list, have the program re-read the directory structure by pulling down the Options menu and pressing D to select the Re-Read the Tree option.

Hiding Directories

Attributes can be assigned to directories with the Modify Attributes function. You can actually hide directories. Select the appropriate attribute by entering the letter shown in bold or a different color.

Hiding a directory

Sorting Directories

You can also sort files according to different criteria with PC Shell. In the directory window, select the directory containing the files to be sorted and displayed. Press Tab to make the file list active. Call the Special menu by pressing S. Select the Directory Sort function by pressing D. A dialog box then requests entry of the sort criteria, as shown in Figure 6.4.

Sorting

You can sort files by name, extension, size, or date and time, or you can sort files according to an order you specify. You may specify whether the files are to be sorted in ascending or descending order.

Enter the number proceeding the chosen sorting field and press the Return key.

The following dialog box provides additional choices. These are:

Confirming sorting

    View   The program displays the sort.

Pressing any key returns the program to the dialog box.

    Resort   Enter new sort criteria.

    Update   The program sorts the directory according to the criteria.

You can sort files within directories and subdirectories, or you can actually sort the directory tree structure. It all

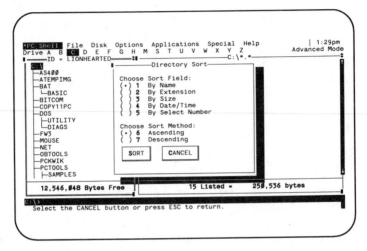

Figure 6.4: The dialog window for entering the sort criteria

depends on which window is active at the time. For example, if you want to sort the directory structure from the root directory on down, you first make the Tree window active. Then you use the cursor keys to highlight the root directory and press S to bring down the Special menu. By selecting the Directory Sort option, you can choose to sort the main directories in alphabetical order. Use the Tab key to select the Update button, then pull down the Options menu and select Re-Read the Tree.

Printing a Directory

Printing

To print the contents of a directory, select the Print Directory function in the File menu. Make sure that the printer is ready. Otherwise the program aborts the function and issues an error message. The program prints out a list of files in the current directory. This list contains file information, including name, extension, file size, date, time, attributes, and number of oc-cupied clusters, regardless of the file display on the screen.

Without appropriate utilities, unintentional deletion of files under MS-DOS or PC-DOS results in the irretrievable loss of important data. In PC Shell the Undelete function restores inadvertently deleted files. In addition, PC Shell has some special functions for monitoring working memory and the hard disk.

Contents

This step shows how to restore inadvertently deleted files. For the sake of brevity, this step shows only automatic restoration, since manual restoration of a deleted file requires detailed knowledge of file structures.

Other special functions of PC Shell are the Mapping options. These provide a graphic display of the file assignment on the data medium. There are other program functions included to check working memory and to display the computer configuration.

Restoring Deleted Files

The Undelete function restores files that have been deleted inadvertently. Files can be completely restored either automatically or manually. However, this can be done only if no new files have been copied or written to the disk. If that has happened, it is likely that the deleted file has been overwritten and can no longer be restored completely. Restore a deleted file as follows:

1. If you delete the file through another program or DOS, do not use the hotkey method to enter PC Shell. Start the program by typing PCSHELL at the DOS prompt.

2. Select the drive and directory containing the deleted file. Start the Undelete function in the Special menu.

Selecting the drive and directory

Confirm that the drive and directory are current with the Return key.

3. Using the Tab key, specify whether to restore a file or a directory. The Create function is also available. Use this function to create a new file using individual sectors. Start the selected function with the Return key.

Selecting file(s)

4. The program displays all deleted files contained in the directory, as shown in Figure 7.1. The "@" character following the file extension shows that automatic restoration is possible. Using the Return key, select the file to be restored. Several files can also be marked. Restoration takes place in the order of marking. Press G or the right mouse button to continue.

Completing file names

5. Enter the first letter of the file name and press the Return key. (See Figure 7.2). You must know the file name in order to restore the file successfully, because deleting a file does not remove it from the disk. Only

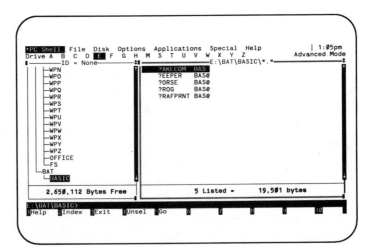

Figure 7.1: Deleted file display

the first letter of the file name is overwritten, indicating to the operating system that the memory space is available. If you have forgotten the name, the file must be restored manually. The Delete Tracking function of the Mirror program described below gets around the need to know the file name.

Start restoration by pressing the Return key again.

6. Select either automatic or manual restoration. Begin the default Automatic function with the Return key.

7. The program displays successful restoration. Then choose the Continue command by pressing the Return key. With this command, you either return to the main menu or restore the next marked file.

To restore a directory completely, select the Subdir function under item 2 and restore the directory. Then, change to this directory, restart the Undelete function and restore the files.

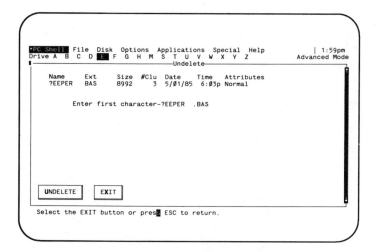

Figure 7.2: Entering the first letter of the file name

The Delete Tracking Function

If you have added Mirror with the /T*n* start-up parameter (where *n* is the drive letter) to your AUTOEXEC.BAT file, information about deleted files will be stored in a file. When starting the Undelete function, the program determines whether such a file exists. It then asks whether to use the information in this file. Select the Del Track function. Then mark the files you wish to restore. Here, you do not have to know the initial letter because Mirror has stored this information. This way, restoration is much simpler and more reliable.

Checking Organization of the Hard Disk

Hard disk organization

If you delete files often and copy new programs to the hard disk, file fragmentation is likely. The operating system does not store files in adjacent areas, but rather distributes them over two or more areas. This results in lengthy access times that increase with the number of fragments.

Choose the Disk Map function in the Special menu to examine the hard disk. The function displays the allocation of the hard disk, allowing analysis of its status at a glance. If allocated and free areas are distributed over the entire hard disk, use the Compress program to reorganize it.

Checking File Allocation

File allocation

The Special menu has a File Map function in addition to the Disk Map function. This function allows viewing the arrangement of individual files on the hard disk, as shown in Figure 7.3 Use this function when file access becomes increasingly slower. This way, you can see quickly whether the file is stored in nonadjacent areas of the hard disk.

Before calling the function, select the directory containing the file and mark it with the cursor bar.

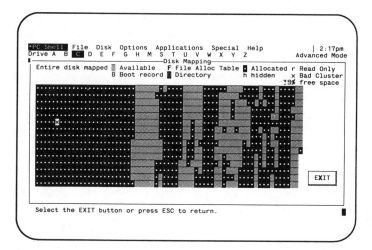

Figure 7.3: The File Map function

The Prior and Next commands allow examination of additional files. Use Prior to move back one file, and Next to see the next file.

Memory Map

Use the Memory Map function to examine working memory. This function not only identifies memory-resident programs, but also determines the blocks of memory they occupy and the interrupt vectors they use.

Working memory

The program has four different examination alternatives available:

1. Shows only the memory areas occupied by programs.

2. Also shows hooked vectors.

3. Shows all memory blocks.

4. Shows all memory blocks and hooked vectors.

Enter the number preceding the appropriate option and press the Return key. The representation differs somewhat depending upon the display selected, but the display contains both the program name and the memory address for all options.

The display of hooked vectors is helpful whenever specific programs operate properly individually, but no longer work properly or do not work at all in combination with other programs.

To return to the main menu, press the X key. To make other memory checks, return to the starting menu of the Memory Map function by pressing M or the Return key.

System Info

System information

The System Info function contained in the Special menu displays all important system data. It displays, among other items, the number of I/O ports and the processor type, and even a speed comparison between your computer and an IBM XT. This function also displays the available memory, the video adapter type and other system information.

Step 8

PC Backup

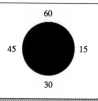

PC Backup is a powerful program for securing data. It has all the facilities offered by much more expensive backup programs, including tape backup support. PC Backup has three different user levels. In this book it will be assumed that the Advanced User level is being used; it is beyond the scope of this book to explore each user level in depth.

Contents

In this step, you will learn how to save files with PC Backup and, in an emergency, how to restore these files back to the hard disk. You will also become acquainted with the different options available for preparing backup floppy disks. You will be introduced to the tape drive backup and restore procedures. If you have already used previous versions of PC Backup, remember that they are not compatible with this new version.

Calling PC Backup

PC Backup can either be called from PC Shell or started from the DOS prompt as follows:

Starting the program

```
PCBACKUP <Return>
```

The program takes a few minutes to read in the directory structure, then the main menu appears. The interface structure is similar to PC Shell, with a few significant differences.

The Horizontal menu bar (shown in Figure 8.1) contains the pull-down menus. You are already familiar with these from PC Shell. The Backup Specification box and user level show the source and destination drives and the current user level. The main portion of the user interface consists of the directory and file windows.

User Interface

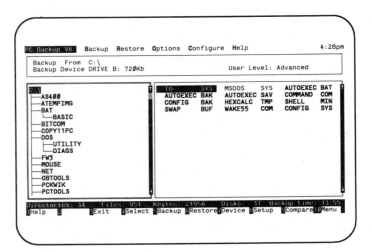

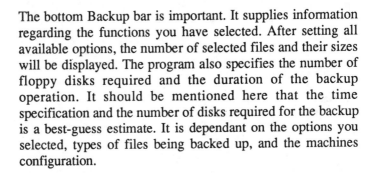

Figure 8.1: The PC Backup user interface

The bottom Backup bar is important. It supplies information regarding the functions you have selected. After setting all available options, the number of selected files and their sizes will be displayed. The program also specifies the number of floppy disks required and the duration of the backup operation. It should be mentioned here that the time specification and the number of disks required for the backup is a best-guess estimate. It is dependant on the options you selected, types of files being backed up, and the machines configuration.

Basic Configuration

Creating the con- figuration

Before backing up data for the first time, you must provide PC Backup with all the necessary information about the source and destination drives. (If you are using PC Backup for the first time, you will automatically be prompted to specify your equipment.) The program saves this information so that the program retains all the settings for the next time it is called.

Specifying the Source Drive

Select the Backup from entry function in the Backup menu and specify the source drive. To back up only a specific directory, specify the appropriate path when identifying the drive as well.

Specifying the Backup Method

Next, select the Backup method function in the Options menu and then specify the backup method. The following choices are available:

Full	The program backs up all selected directories and the files contained within them, changing the archive bit accordingly.
Full Copy	The program also backs up all selected files. However, it does not change the archive bit.
Incremental	The program backs up only files changed since the last data backup. It clears the archive bit. The Incremental backup will merge the history file with that of the Full backup resulting in one history file.
Separate Incremental	The program backs up only the files changed since the last backup. However it keeps its own history file and does not append to the one on the full backup. The archive bit is cleared.
Differential	Backs up only those files that have not been backed up since the last Full backup. It does not clear the archive bit.

Select the desired function with the cursor keys and then confirm the choice with the Return key.

Selecting the Disk Type and Backup Method

Defining the destination disks

In the Configure menu, call the Define Equipment function by pressing F8. Then specify the capacity of the existing disk drives. If you have a tape drive supported by PC Backup, you will be presented with a choice to define it here.

After selecting the backup mode, choose the OK command with the Tab key and confirm this command with the Return key. This option can also be selected with the combination of the Alt key and the key shown in bold or a different color.

Specifying the Destination Drive and Media Type

To specify the destination drive and media type call the Choose drive and Media function in the Configure menu by pressing the F7 key. Make the selection with the cursor keys, press the Tab key to OK and confirm the choice with the Return key.

Starting the Backup

Once you have selected the basic settings, begin the file backup operation by choosing the Start Backup function in the Backup menu. You can also start the backup operation with the F5 key. A dialog box will appear prompting you to enter a backup description and password. You may choose to use these options or just press the Alt-O key combination to skip them.

During the file backup operation, you need only insert new floppy disks. The program will normally sense the disk insertion and will continue the backup without any more user input. If the program does not recognize the disk insertion, then confirm with the Return key. Upon completion, a status window appears. It displays how many files the program backed up, how many floppy disks it took, and how much time elapsed.

To exit the program, press F3 and then X to confirm to exit either to the operating system prompt or to PC Shell.

More Detailed Configuration

Besides the basic configuration, PC Backup has additional functions for selecting files. This can simplify the selection of files to be backed up. The program even provides for file compression. This option can save a considerable amount of space required on floppy disks, however it does take more time to complete the actual backup.

The program has a new option for error correction. It saves additional information about the backed up files on the floppy disks, so that if damage to a disk occurs after the backup is complete, you still have a good chance of successfully restoring the data. The Error correction is on unless you specify otherwise.

Individual Files/Directory Selection

The Choose directories function found in the Backup menu helps to select individual files. As an alternative, you may call this function at any time with the F4 key. As in PC Shell, you can switch between the directory and file windows with the Tab key. The default is to select all subdirectories and files, but you may exclude the appropriate directories and files by highlighting them with the cursor keys and pressing the Return key (see Figure 8.2). Files tagged for backup

*Directory/
file
selection*

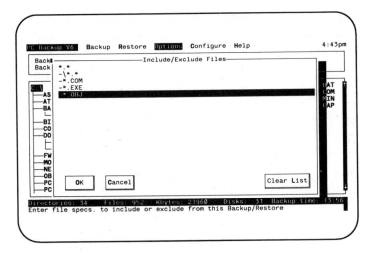

Figure 8.2: Selecting file groups

are highlighted by the program. Make sure the Backup status bar confirms what you think you see. The highlights can be misleading.

Backing Up Subdirectories

Sub-directories

If you also wish to back up subdirectories, select the Subdirectory inclusion function in the Options menu. The default provides for the backup of subdirectories. Select this function to switch it off. You can see whether or not subdirectories will be backed up by looking at the character preceding the function name. If a check mark is present, Subdirectory inclusion is on.

Including or Excluding File Groups

File groups

Specific file groups can be included or excluded with the Include/exclude files function.

Up to 16 file groups may be included or excluded by entering their names or their file extensions. End each line with the Return key. For example, to include all files with a .TXT extension in the backup, enter the following:

```
*.TXT      <Return>
```

However, the best use of this function is to exclude specific file groups. First, make sure that all files are selected by typing *.* in the first line and pressing the Return key. If you wish to deselect a file group use the "-" character. The program will exclude the specified file group. To exclude files with .COM or .EXE extensions, enter the file groups as follows:

```
*.*        <Return>
-*.COM     <Return>
-*.EXE     <Return>
```

Once you have made the choice, confirm it with the Alt-O key combination. As an alternative, start the desired command with the Tab key followed by the Return key. All entries can be deleted using the Clear List option. Make sure you specify the "*.*" selection again in the first position. Otherwise, errors may occur when exiting the function.

Excluding Files According to Attributes

Normally, all hidden files and system files are excluded during backup. With the Attribute exclusions function, you can specify whether the program should also back up these files. In addition, you can specify that files with the Read only attribute are to be excluded from the backup.

File attribute

However, remember when backing up copy-protected files that these attributes are often part of a copy protection scheme. These files could be damaged when the program backs them up to floppy disk, or it may not be possible to restore them properly to the hard disk. Check your software manuals for appropriate instructions.

Selection by Date

File date

To specify files for backup by date, select the Date range selection function in the Options menu, and then proceed as follows:

1. Using the cursor keys, specify whether the files are to be selected by date and then press the Return key.

2. Press the Tab key to enter the time period.

3. End the selection with the Alt-O key combination.

Compressing Files

File compression

The Compress function provides two different compression methods, each having an effect on backup duration and the number of disks required. Start the function in the Options menu and select from among the following choices:

None	No compression.
Minimize Disks	Requires fewer floppy disks but the backup duration increases. Compression is between 10–60%.
Minimize Time	Minimal compression takes place. On slow computers compression may not often take place. Compression will not occur if it will significantly increase the backup duration.

Select the desired option with the cursor keys and confirm the choice with the Alt-O key combination.

Verifying Files

To be certain that the target disks have no damaged clusters, select the Verify function in the Options menu. Three different possibilities are available:

None	No verification.
When formatting	Verifies only when formatting floppy disks for the first backup in DMA mode.
Always	Verifies for every backup.

Verifying

Formatting Floppy Disks

If you choose the faster DMA mode, the program reformats the floppy disks for the first backup. The Format function makes it possible to choose whether floppy disks are to be formatted only as needed or for every backup operation.

Protecting Files Against Overwriting

The Overwrite warning function prevents inadvertent overwriting of existing backup files on floppy disks. When restoring files from a backup, the program will ask you whether you wish to overwrite existing files. You can select this function through the Options menu.

Saving the Configuration

Once you have made all settings, save them with the Save as default function in the Configure menu. When you next call the program, the selected configuration is again available. You will then no longer need to enter complicated configuration data when restoring backup floppy disks.

Saving the settings

Generating an Individual Configuration

The Save setup function found in the Options menu stores different configurations. Files hold these configurations and you may call them as needed. For example, you can store a comprehensive setting to back up all files this way. You can then call this configuration at the end of each week. In addition, you can create another setting to back up only updated files that you access every day. With a setup file you can ran PC Backup from the command line as follows:

PCBACKUP BACKUP1 <Return>

(where *BACKUP1* is the setup file name)

An individual configuration is stored as follows:

1. After you have selected your settings, press the Alt-S key combination.

2. Enter a file name and store it with the Alt-O key combination.

In order to reload a stored setting, proceed as follows:

1. Press Alt-L and, with the cursor keys, select the desired configuration from those shown in the window.

2. Load the setting with the Alt-O key combination.

Another possible use of this feature arises when several people use the same computer. Each person can then store his or her individual configuration to back up only their own files on the hard disk.

Restoring Backup Floppy Disks

Restore

If you ever need to restore the backup floppy disks, pull down the Restore menu and select the Restore to entry function. Here, enter only the destination drive. If you have saved the configuration when backing up files, you need only select the Start Restore function and insert the backup floppy disks one after another as the program prompts you.

If someone has backed up the data according to an individual setting, load the file containing the configuration data with the Alt-L key combination and then start restoring the data.

To restore certain files only, specify the selection criteria as when making the backup floppy disks. The same functions are available and the operation is identical. These functions are useful whenever there are lost files only in specific directories. If you can no longer restore the lost data with the PC Shell Undelete function, select the corresponding files and copy them back onto the hard disk.

Verifying Backup Floppy Disks

You can check the floppy disks generated by PC Backup using its DOS-compatible mode with the DOS DIR command. This will only let you see the two file names PC Backup created to store your file information.

You can compare the files you just backed up with the originals on the hard drive using the Compare command or you can compare anytime after you do backup, as long as you have a history file. The Save History function is on by default. This function is found in the Options menu.

Comparing Files

1. Select the Choose Directories option in the Restore menu.

2. When the history files appear, specify which one you wish to use. Then select OK.

3. The Tree list and the File list will display the information in the backup history file.

4. Now choose the Start compare option from the Restore menu. You will be prompted to insert the appropriate backup floppy disks. The program will verify file-by-file the data on the disks. It is highly recommended that you perform this function. This advice goes for any other backup program also.

While comparing you may see some of the following symbols:

=   The files are an identical match.

<   The backup file is older than the file on the hard disk, but the files are identical.

<<   The backup file is older than the file on the hard disk, but they are not identical.

>   The backup file is newer than the file on the hard disk, but they are identical.

>>   The backup file is newer than the file on the hard disk, but they are not identical.

s   The size of the backup file is different than the one on the hard disk, however the date and time are the same.

−   The backup file is not on the hard disk.

x   The backup file is not identical to the file on the hard disk.

Tape Backups

*Config-
uring PC
Backup*

If you have a tape drive supported by PC Backup you will have additional options both in the Define Equipment dialog box and the Choose drive and Media dialog box.

Specify in the Choose drive and Media dialog box that you wish to do a tape backup. Use the cursor keys to highlight the appropriate tape capacity entry and press the Return key. Use the Tab key to select OK and confirm by pressing the Return key.

To start the Backup, use the following procedures:

1. Select Start Backup in the Backup menu or press the F5 key. You will be prompted to insert a tape cartridge. This may take some time, possibly up to a minute. The message bar at the bottom of the screen tells you what is happening.

2. A dialog box will appear listing all the backups contained on the cartridge. You may elect to begin this new backup immediately after the last one, or you can choose to erase the previous backup. Use the Tab key to make your selection and confirm with the Return key.

3. Another dialog box will appear prompting you for a description and a password. You may choose to use these options or just press Alt-O to start the backup procedure.

Comparing Data on a Tape Backup

You can compare the files backed up to the tape drive with the original files on the hard drive. This operation is recommended to ensure a good backup.

Comparing data

To start:

1. Select the Choose Directories option in the Restore menu. You can then specify which backup set to use in the comparision. Highlight your choice and select OK.

2. The Tree list and File list windows are updated. Start the Compare function from the Restore menu. You will see the bar scanning across the File list window. It

will leave the appropriate code to let you know the status of the comparison.

To restore files from a tape drive is essentially the same as comparing the files, except you are writing to the hard drive. To perform a restore operation, do the following:

1. Select the Restore to Entry option in the Restore menu. A dialog box will appear. Type in the drive and path to specify the destination of the restored files. If the drive and path are correct already, just select OK by pressing Alt-O.

2. Select the Start restore function located on the Restore menu.

Step 9

Compress

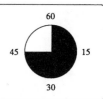

Compress is a powerful hard disk reorganization program that will unfragment files and relocate the files to the front of the disk. This minimizes hard-disk read-head movements and accelerates file access. This step will show how to analyze the hard disk with the aid of Compress. You will then see how to improve access speed by reorganizing any fragmentation of file allocation.

Starting Compress

Before calling Compress, it is wise to remove all memory-resident programs that are loaded. Memory-resident programs may cause complications during the reorganization of the hard disk. If you wish to remove PC Shell and Desktop from working memory, use the Kill program, and then start Compress from the DOS prompt by typing:

```
COMPRESS <Return>
```

To start Compress from PC Shell while in nonresident mode, select the program from the Applications menu.

Compress has a similar interface to PC Shell, and you control it in much the same manner. However, there are no windows here providing information about files or directories. You see only a graphic representation of the allocation of individual clusters of the hard disk (see Figure 9.1). You will see the occupied and free blocks of the disk at a glance. If there are single free clusters between occupied blocks, these usually represent fragmented files. The operating system reads these files more slowly than files stored in one contiguous block. The program also displays damaged areas that have already been marked by a low level format. The surface analysis portion of the program will check for areas that have not yet

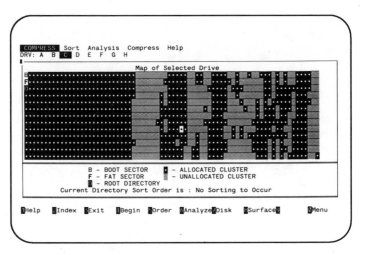

Figure 9.1: The user interface of Compress

been marked as bad. If these areas are not marked as bad, then DOS may store data there that will become corrupted.

Analyzing a Hard Disk

Analysis

Before starting the process of organizing the hard disk, check the status of the hard disk using the analysis programs of Compress. You should do this because the process of organizing the disk can be very time consuming and can last up to two hours for a 20 Mb hard disk. These Compress options examine the hard disk from various points of view and suggest whether reorganization is necessary.

File Allocation Information

File allocation

Call the Disk analysis function in the Analysis menu or press the F7 key. This program function examines the hard disk for file allocation. After a few moments, it also provides information in a window regarding the state of the disk, as shown in Figure 9.2.

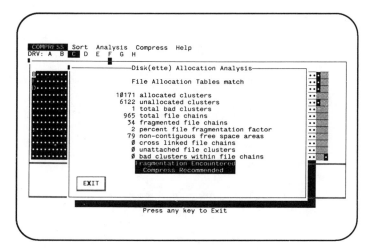

Figure 9.2: The file allocation display

This displays the number of allocated clusters of the hard disk, whether blocks are damaged, and whether fragmented files exist. The display showing single clusters not allocated to any file is particularly important.

If this program displays such clusters, exit Compress by pressing the Esc key and call the MS-DOS or PC-DOS CHKDSK utility with the /f switch. CHKDSK then converts lost portions of files into files. As an alternative, you can use Diskfix to clear up any lost clusters (see Step 10). Use PC Shell to identify these portions of files. Step 5 describes how to edit files.

File Analysis

Check for any fragmentation of individual files using the File analysis option in the Analysis menu. If you find files not stored in contiguous blocks while examining the hard disk, you may use this function to determine which files are involved.

File analysis

The analysis provides information regarding the number of clusters allocated for each file, the number of areas used to store each file, and the percentage of fragmentation (see Figure 9.3).

Specifying a directory

The following commands are available to examine all directories. Select the command by entering the letter shown in reverse video.

PREV DIR	One directory backward at the same level.
NEXT DIR	One directory forward at the same level.
FIRST DIR	Choose the main directory
LAST DIR	Choose the last directory
EXIT	Return to the main menu

Cluster Analysis

The third analysis function checks all clusters on the selected disk. It also marks clusters that, although not damaged

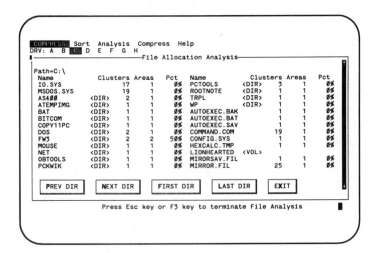

Figure 9.3: File analysis

enough to be recognized by the operating system, may still cause data loss. After marking, data will no longer be stored in these clusters. Such data will then not be lost in a subsequent cluster failure.

Select the Surface analysis function in the Analysis menu or press F8 to start cluster analysis. Once you have called the function, specify the number of passes. If you do not have much time, specify a single pass because the program takes a while to scan the whole disk surface. It is, however, recommended that you let Surface analysis run continuously overnight. This will afford the best results when searching for marginal or bad clusters. You can print out the results of the examination on a printer or write them to a file to be read later using the PC Shell editor.

Sorting Files

Before starting to reorganize, select the sorting functions in the Sort menu. You will use these functions to sort the files in the individual directories. Select the Sort menu by pressing S.

Sorting

Specify the sorting sequence by entering the letter of the appropriate function shown in reverse video. The menu provides the following functions:

Date/Time	Sort by date and time
File name	Sort by file name
Extension	Sort by file extension
Size	Sort by size

You also specify whether the files are to be sorted in ascending or descending order. You may choose to ignore sorting options altogether because options have a significant effect on the duration of the reorganization.

Specifying the Organization Type

Hard-disk organi- zation

You may select from three different levels of organization. To specify a method, pull down the Compress menu and set the desired function using the cursor bar and the Return key. The selected function is identified by a check mark preceding its name.

Unfragment only	Eliminates all fragmentation.
Full Compression	Writes all allocated clusters to one contiguous block in the front of the hard disk while unfragmenting.
Full Compression/Clear	Eliminates all fragmentation, separates allocated and free clusters and overwrites all free clusters. After reorganizing the hard disk, you can no longer restore deleted files. This function is the most thorough and most precise facility for organizing a hard disk. It will take quite awhile. For this reason, call this function only when you can afford the time.

Hard Disk Allocation

Hard disk structure

The Ordering Options function in the Compress menu provides four different alternatives for allocating the hard disk. Position the cursor bar on the desired option and press the Return key to specify the function. The following choices are available:

Standard	During reorganization, this places files wherever there is sufficient disk space available.

.COM & .EXE FIRST   Writes all files having an extension of .COM and .EXE to a contiguous block in the front (first) tracks of the hard disk. You can select this function if you do not erase program files often. This is because fragmentation occurs rarely or not at all in the front area of the hard disk. Later Compressions proceed substantially faster because the front portion of the hard disk need not be reorganized each time.

DOS w/Sub   Writes all subdirectories to the front of the disk, then arranges the files by directory. This function reduces the time required for disk accesses because fewer tracks need to be read.

DOS w/Sub and Files   Writes a directory and its contents in contiguous blocks, then writes another directory and its contents, and so on, until the whole hard disk is in contiguous blocks located near the front of the disk.

Function-Dependent Hard Disk Analysis

The Compress menu provides an additional context-sentitive function for analyzing the hard disk. You must first select a type of organization and only then can you call this function. Based on the previously specified organization criteria, the Analyze Disk Organization function checks whether reorganization is necessary at all and displays an appropriate message.

Printing a Report

Printing

In addition to the screen display of the reorganized hard disk, you can send the most important data to a printer or to a text file. To do this, select the Print Report function in the Compress menu. A menu provides a choice between output to the printer or to a file. Select the desired output by entering the letter shown in bold or a different color. The printout contains information regarding the organization type, time used, and the number of free and allocated clusters.

Starting Reorganization

After selecting all desired functions, select the Begin Compress option in the Compress menu or press F4. Depending upon the state of the hard disk and the selections chosen, you may now take a break from the computer. As a precaution, turn the brightness down to prevent burn-in. Once the operation has finished, the program displays the new allocation of the hard disk. The program has now located all files in contiguous blocks and arranged the free clusters in one contiguous block. The only exception to this is hidden or system files. The Compress program will not move these files, because their operation may depend upon a specific location on the hard disk. Once the program is through, it will give you opportunity to run the Mirror program. It is strongly advised to reboot the computer, so all the file pointers get reset in the File Allocation Table.

Startup Parameters

Parameters

Instead of selecting the individual functions in the various menus, you may also initially specify the necessary functions as startup parameters. Here are the main parameters that are available:

Start-up parameters	Effect
/NM	Does not call Mirror.
/CU	Starts the Unfragment only option.
/CF	Starts the Full Compression option.
/CC	Starts the Full Compression-Clear option.
/SF	Sorts by file name.
/ST	Sorts by time.
/SE	Sorts by file extension.
/SS	Sorts by file size.
/SA	Sorts in ascending order.
/SD	Sorts in descending order.
/OS	Provides standard organization.
/OD	Puts directories in contiguous blocks.
/OP	Writes .COM and .EXE files to the front area of the hard disk.

Copy-protected Programs

Many copy-protected programs work with files having hidden and system attributes. As noted above, Compress does not move these files because this might cause the programs to stop functioning. As an added precaution, check whether your software might be damaged by Compress.

Step 10

Diskfix

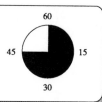

Diskfix is a utility that will let you repair most common problems afflicting hard disks and floppy disks, and it is easy to use, because it is automatic, requiring little user interaction. If you have problems accessing a hard disk or floppy disk, Diskfix will help out. It can also be used in a regular maintenance program for the hard drive.

In this step you will learn to how to call Diskfix and what prompts to answer. You will find out which situations merit using the Diskfix utility.

Starting the Diskfix Program

Although you can call Diskfix from PC Shell while it is resident in memory, it is strongly recommended that no memory-resident programs be loaded at the time. Memory-resident programs may interfere with Diskfix's operation. The only exception would be mouse drivers or hard disk drivers. To begin, type at the DOS prompt:

```
Diskfix <Return>
```

Diskfix will do an extensive test of the system's BIOS, CMOS (found on 286/386 machines), the partition table, and all logical boot sector data. It may take a few seconds. If a problem is encountered, Diskfix will display an error dialog box with the symptoms listed and the suggested course of action. If no problem is detected, a message will appear asking, "Do you want to repair a disk now?" as in Figure 10.1.

Answering yes will begin the program's diagnostic checks; otherwise Diskfix will present you with a menu containing

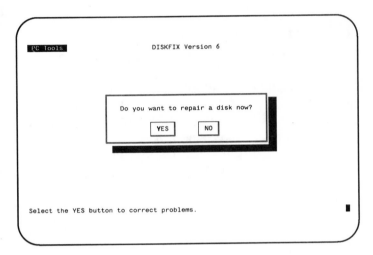

Figure 10.1: Automatic Analysis dialog box

four options, as shown in Figure 10.2:

Fix a Disk   Starts the automatic diagnostic and repair routine.

Surface Scan   Scans the disk cluster-by-cluster for corruption and read errors. If a read error is encountered, the cluster will be marked as bad in the file allocation table so DOS will not use it. If the cluster is allocated, Diskfix will read as much of the data as possible and move it to a safe cluster. Any data that is not readable will have dashes (–) substituted instead. This will allow the user to identify the damaged area. Executable files will not benefit much from this, but it is invaluable for data files.

Note: This is much like Surface Analysis in the Compress program, but far superior in damaged file and disk recovery.

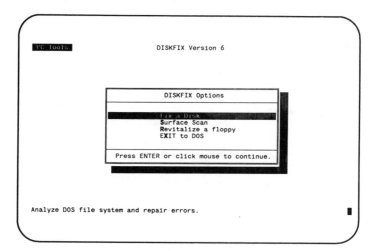

```
  PC Tools              DISKFIX Version 6


                ┌──────────────────────────────┐
                │        DISKFIX Options        │
                ├──────────────────────────────┤
                │        Fix a Disk             │
                │        Surface Scan           │
                │        Revitalize a floppy    │
                │        EXIT to DOS            │
                ├──────────────────────────────┤
                │ Press ENTER or click mouse to continue. │
                └──────────────────────────────┘



 Analyze DOS file system and repair errors.              ■
```

Figure 10.2: Diskfix main menu

Revitalize a floppy   Allows Diskfix to read a floppy with sector errors when DOS refuses to read them. Diskfix reads floppies differently than DOS, therefore it is able to refresh weak areas that DOS balks at. It reads the data track-by-track into memory, then reformats the disk, and finally recopies the original data back to the disk (see Figure 10.3). A graphic screen shows you the progress Diskfix is making.

Fixing a Disk

Fix a disk

When you choose to fix a disk, the program will ask you which drive you wish to check. A dialog window will appear. Scroll with the cursor keys until you highlight the desired drive and press the Return key. If you are checking a floppy be sure you insert it before selecting the drive. While Diskfix

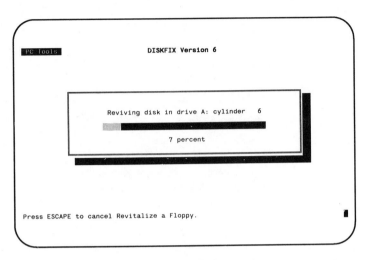

Figure 10.3: Revitalizing a floppy disk

examines the disk it will display a window of what it is testing (see Figure 10.4).

The following areas are tested:

DOS boot sector	Every floppy has a boot sector, whether it is bootable or not. Diskfix checks to see if the information stored here is damaged in any way.
Media descriptors	DOS uses a special byte to tell the system what kind of disk the floppy is. DOS stores the byte in the file allocation table (FAT). Diskfix verifies that this information is correct for the type of drive being analyzed.
File Allocation Table	Diskfix verifies that both copies of the FAT are readable, identical,

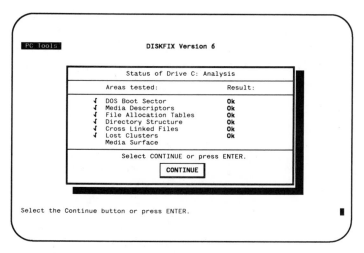

Figure 10.4: Diskfix Status window

and have no invalid entries. If one copy is readable while the other is not, Diskfix will copy the readable copy of the FAT over the corrupted copy.

Directory structure   Diskfix makes sure the directory data is readable and correct. It looks for illegal file names, file sizes, cross-linked files, and FAT errors.

Cross linked files   Files that have been allocated the same address in the FAT are called cross-linked files. Diskfix will try to determine what clusters belong to what files. It will attempt repairs based on what it finds.

Lost subdirectories   Diskfix will ask whether you wish to search for lost subdirectories. If you do, it will look for data that appears to be a subdirectory entry. This search will take a few minutes. Note: This option should be used with caution, since it is possible to recover subdirectories from past formats.

Lost Clusters   Like the DOS CHKDSK/F program, Disk-fix can find and convert files to lost clusters. If you choose to convert the data to files, they will have the file name and extension of PCT00000.FIX, PCT00001.FIX, and so on. You can view these files through a file editor to determine if the data is valuable or not.

When a problem is encountered, Diskfix will display a description of the problem and a course of action. You do not need to be a programmer to make an intelligent decision in this regard. You just choose Yes or No to Diskfix's suggestions.

Types of Errors Diskfix Corrects

Errors corrected by Diskfix

The following is a list of some of the errors Diskfix was designed to remedy.

File not found	Abort, Retry, Ignore, Fail
Bad command or file name	Cannot find system file
Error Writing Fixed Disk	File Allocation Table bad, drive *x* Abort, Retry, Ignore, Fail
Invalid Current Directory	Invalid Drive specification

Diskfix, along with the other PC Tools utilities, should be used in a regular maintenance program for your hard disk and floppies. It is always best to catch a problem before it gets out of control, and Diskfix will help in safeguarding your data from possible corruption.

Mirror/Rebuild

An inadvertently formatted hard disk is one of the worst dis-
asters that a PC user can imagine. With older DOS versions,
this happens more often than you think.

In this step, you will learn how to restore an accidentally formatted hard disk or floppy disk using the Mirror and Rebuild
programs.

Mirror

Mirror and Rebuild do not have the same interface as the
other programs. They can be called from PC Shell or from
the DOS prompt. You should install the Mirror program in
your AUTOEXEC.BAT file, because this is the only way to
obtain the best error-free restoration. Mirror stores information about your files in two files, named MIRROR.FIL and
MIRRORSAV.FIL. These files are retained following an inadvertent format and ensure restoration of the disk. In order
to install Mirror manually, call the program from the DOS
prompt:

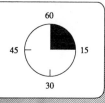

```
MIRROR n:
```

Replace the letter *n* with the designation of the drive where
Mirror is to store the file information. To add Mirror to the
AUTOEXEC.BAT file later, use an ASCII file editor to insert
the program call following the path specification.

*Starting
the
program*

File Deletion Record

For greater reliability in protecting files against unintentional
deletion, Mirror also has the Delete Tracking function. With
this, the reconstruction of deleted files using the Undelete option in PC Shell is quite easy. By using the start-up parameter

*Delete
Tracking*

/T*n* (where *n* is the drive letter), information regarding deleted files on the designated disk is stored in a file named PCTRACKER.DEL. Mirror always puts this file in the main directory. The size of the file depends on the type of drive used, but it may be individually configured. Depending on the size, the program stores information regarding the appropriate number of files. The following sizes are the defaults:

Data medium	File size	Number of entries
360K	5K	25
720K	9K	50
1.2Mb	14K	75
1.44Mb	14K	75
20Mb	18K	101
32Mb	36K	202
greater than 32Mb	55K	303

When starting, call Mirror with the /T*n* switch. In this switch, the letter n stands for the drive identifier. To increase or decrease the number of entries in the file, specify the start-up switch /T*n-nnn*. Here, enter the number of desired entries in place of the string *nnn*.

Rebuild

Rebuild returns inadvertently formatted hard disks and floppy disks to their original state. However, this only works reliably if you used Mirror to store all the file information and you formatted with PC Format. Restoration on a hard disk will succeed even if you used the DOS Format program, provided you have used Mirror. If you did not use the Mirror program previously, restoration without errors is rarely possible.

Be aware, however, that there are a few manufacturer-specific DOS versions that will overwrite all data on the hard disk. The Mirror program and Rebuild will not be able to recover from such a format. Compaq DOS version 3.2 is a good example of a destructive format. Check your DOS manual or ask your dealer if you are in doubt.

Formatted floppy disks can be restored only if you used PC Format to do the job. DOS Format is destructive in that it overwrites all previous data. This is why PC Setup renames the DOS Format command to FORMAT!.COM to help prevent such a serious mistake.

Starting the Program

Call the program from the DOS prompt:

```
REBUILD n:
```

As for Mirror, the letter *n* identifies the drive or data medium to be restored. The screen now displays the current Mirror image file and the previous Mirror image file create by the Mirror program. Press L to restore the current state. Otherwise, pressing the P key causes the program to restore to the previous state. An additional safety prompt that allows you to abort the program then follows. Press N to cancel formatting.

Never test the Rebuild program without a compelling reason (inadvertent formatting). If the last mirror image file of the file allocation table is already old, you will not be able to restore the current state of the hard disk. You will be able to restore the state at the time Mirror was last run, yet you may lose important data this way. The best safeguard is to have a good current backup on hand.

Saving Partition Information

If you have ever received the message *Invalid drive specification* when attempting to access your hard disk, it is very probable that the partition table of the drive has been destroyed. Mirror allows you to store this partition information on a floppy disk. If you can no longer access the hard disk, something that occurs very rarely, you can restore the hard drive's Partition Table with the information stored on the floppy disk. To save the Partition Table, call Mirror as follows:

```
MIRROR /PARTN
```

Please be aware that the Mirror program is purely a DOS utility, therefore it can only record partitions made by the DOS FDISK program. Mirror will ask you to insert a formatted floppy. Keep this floppy disk handy because the Rebuild/Partn option requires this disk. The program stores all partition information in a file named PARTNSAV.FIL. Store this floppy disk in a safe place.

Restoring the Partition Table

To restore the hard disk in the event the partition information was destroyed, call Rebuild, again with the /PARTN start-up switch. The program requests the floppy disk generated with Mirror /PARTN. Rebuild then restores the previous state of the hard disk using the stored partition information.

Step 12

PC Secure

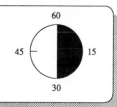

Contents

If several users share a PC, it may be advisable that not all users be allowed access to all the files. PC Secure serves to encode files or entire subdirectories. These can then only be decoded again after entry of a password.

In this step, you will learn how to select a file or directory and protect it against unauthorized access with a password. Options for providing increased security are also available.

Restrictions

Versions of PC Tools Deluxe obtained outside the USA contain a slimmed-down version of the original PC Secure program. It is illegal to export the program that encodes files using the DES algorithm. For this reason, such versions contain only a file compression program.

Starting the Program

The program can be called from the DOS prompt like this:

*Starting
the
program*

```
PCSECURE   <Return>
```

You have a number of parameters available for starting the program. These are:

/BW   To display on a monochrome screen while using CGA video card.

/350   May be needed on a system equipped with a VGA video adapter.

/G   Used if you have need of tight file security, like that required by the U.S. Department of Defense.

This is known as the DOD standard. Any file encrypted while this parameter is in effect will have its original file destroyed by being overwritten seven times, then verified as to the success of the destruction.

Master Key

Master key

When PC Secure is called for the first time, the program requests entry of a master password known as the *key*, as shown in Figure 12.1. With this password, you can decrypt files for which users have forgotten the individual password. It is the backdoor to file decryption.

After entering the password, you must enter it a second time as confirmation. Then the program adds it to the executable program file. Save the master password somewhere that only you have access and be sure not to forget it.

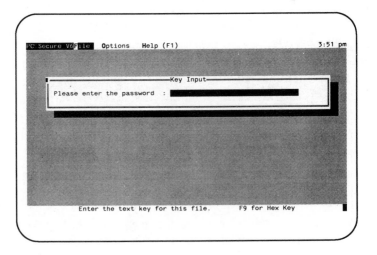

Figure 12.1: Entering the master password

Encrypting a File

To encrypt a single file only, proceed as follows:

1. Change to the directory containing the file and start PC Secure. You will be presented with a menu at the top of the screen. At the bottom of the screen are function keys used to call the options. Press F4 to encrypt a file.

2. The file selection window now displays all files contained in the selected directory (see Figure 12.2). Move the cursor bar to the file.

3. As the Encrypt File function is already active, you need only press the Return key.

4. Now enter an individual password. You will be asked to enter it a second time to confirm it. If you make a typing error, the program aborts, and you must enter the desired password again.

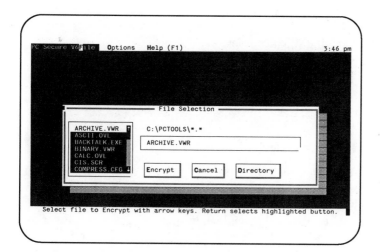

Figure 12.2: The PC Secure file selection window

5. Once the program has encoded the file, return to the main menu with the Esc key.

6. To end PC Secure, select the Exit function in the File menu. Confirm by pressing Return.

The encoded file now has the same name but can no longer be accessed. ASCII files are not readable, program files cannot be executed. If you attempt to run an encrypted program file, it may "hang" the computer, requiring a reboot.

Encrypting Directories

Directories

You can also encrypt entire directories with all their associated files, just as you did for individual files. To protect a directory against unauthorized access, mark it in the file selection window with the cursor bar, then select the Directory function with the Tab key. When the Return key is pressed, the program requests confirmation. Use the Tab key to select OK. You can also include the subdirectories in the encryption process by pressing I. Pressing the I key a second time excludes the subdirectories.

Enter the password and confirm by entering it a second time. After the program encrypts the files, a window displays a message stating how many files have been encrypted.

Decrypting Files

To decrypt an encrypted file, call PC Secure while in the directory containing the file. Press F5 to decrypt and position the cursor bar over the file name. Start the Decrypt function with the Return key and begin decrypting the file. Enter the password used to encrypt the file, and verify it by entering the password a second time. If the password is correctly entered, the program will return the file to its original state. If an incorrect password is entered, an error message is displayed. You must start again from the beginning. If you have forgotten the password, decode the file using the master password.

Decrypting Directories

Decrypting a directory follows the same pattern used for an individual file. Call the Decrypt function by pressing F5 and mark the directory with the cursor bar. Choose the Directory function with the Alt-D key combination. Decide whether you want any encrypted subdirectories also decrypted. Begin decrypting the files by selecting OK with the Tab key and pressing the Return key. Enter the password and confirm it. Once the process finishes, return to the main menu with the Esc key.

Options

PC Secure contains a few functions that affect the type of encryption and increase the protection against unauthorized access. Select these functions in the Options menu by entering the letter shown in bold or a different color or with the cursor bar. A check mark preceding the name indicates whether a function is active or not. Calling these options works like a toggle switch. When the function is first called, it is enabled. When it is called again, it is disabled.

Compressing Files

The Compression function causes a compression of the files to be encrypted. This process saves space. The savings can range from a few percent up to about 80 percent of the original file size.

One Password for Several Files

Use the One Key function to encrypt several, but not all, files in a directory. If the function is enabled, simply enter a password when encrypting the first file. The program does not prompt for the password again when encrypting any additional files, because it uses the password of the first file. When decrypting, all files are decrypted using this password.

Deleting the Original File

The Delete Original File function deletes the original file. It then destroys the original so it cannot be undeleted. Always use this function if you used the /G parameter to load PC Secure.

Blocking Write Access

The Read-Only function blocks all write accesses to the encrypted data. This prevents accidental deletion by DOS.

Hiding Files

If you do not wish the files to be displayed in the directory, choose the Hidden function to mark the files with the hidden attribute. When the directory contents are listed at the DOS prompt, these files do not appear. However, PC Shell and some other software utilities can even display hidden files.

Expert Mode

The Expert Mode function makes it impossible to use the master password as an additional decryption option. This adds security to your files. *Do not forget your password!*

Saving the Configuration

Store the settings made in the Options menu with the Save Preferences function.

Forgetting the Individual and Master Passwords

If you have forgotten your individual password and Master key, you will not be able decrypt an encrypted file. There is no known way to decode these files without the passwords.

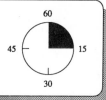

PC-Cache and PC Format do not have the same user interface as the other programs. However, they may be integrated into the interface of PC Shell and called from there.

PC-Cache

PC-Cache is a cache program that accelerates hard disk access by creating an intermediate, or cache memory. It increases the data transfer rate but not the access time of the hard disk. For this reason, you should use it primarily for database and word processing applications. If you have not installed PC-Cache in the AUTOEXEC.BAT file, you can call it at any time from the DOS prompt. However, make sure it is loaded before all applications that transfer files back and forth to the hard drive.

Startup Parameters

PC-Cache has many startup parameters that make it possible to customize the program optimally for your computer.

Startup parameters	Effect
/In	Ignores specific drives, where n stands for drive.
/SIZE=nnnK	Provides a user definable cache buffer.
/SIZEXP=nnnK	Allocates EMS memory.
/SIZEXT=nnnK	Allocates extended memory (greater than 640K).

Startup parameters	Effect
/SIZEXT*=*nnnn*K	PC-Cache determines the best method to access extended memory by checking the CPU and other parameters. This option is seldom needed. It should only be used to force PC-Cache to use the BIOS to access extended memory.
/EXTSTART=*nnnn*K	Specifies starting location of PC-Cache in extended memory. It must be above 1024K.
/FLUSH	Empties the cache memory.
/INFO	Displays information concerning available drives. If PC-Cache is loaded as memory-resident, it must be unloaded to run this feature.
/MAX=*nn*	This specifies the number of sectors that will be cached on a given read request. The larger the application or data file, the smaller the number should be for optimum performance. The default is 4.
/MEASURES	Displays the performance of PC-Cache. It will display physical reads to the hard drive, logical reads to the buffer, transfers saved, and percentage saved.
/PARAM	Displays parameters in effect.
/PARAM*	Displays the setup information of PC-Cache.
/PAUSE	This parameter is like a trace. If you experience problems after

Startup parameters	Effect
	installing PC-Cache use the parameter to track down the problem. Watch the bootup screen for messages and follow the advice displayed.
/QUIET	Disables the boot sign-on display.
/UNLOAD	Unloads PC-Cache from resident memory.
/WRITE=ON/OFF	Controls whether write caching is turned on or off. The default is on. If you experience periodic lockups of the computer set /WRITE=OFF to disable write caching.
/?	Displays all the parameters used by PC-Cache.

Examples

1. PC-Cache /IC /Size=100K—The cache memory has a size of 100K and excludes drive C from accelerated access.

2. PC-Cache /SIZEXP=150K—Creates a 150K cache memory in EMS memory.

PC Format

The PC Format program replaces the DOS FORMAT program. A batch file created during installation and named FORMAT.BAT ensures that you are able to format floppy disks as usual with the FORMAT command. PC Format uses a different formatting method that makes it possible to restore floppy disks that have been formatted inadvertently. Floppy disks need not have been preformatted with PC Format to allow for data recovery. PC Format can be called both from the DOS prompt and from PC Shell. When formatting floppy disks already containing data, the program issues an additional warning regarding the loss of data.

Options

PC Format has various options that can be specified when calling the program.

Option	Effect
/1	Allows for single-sided format.
/4	Formats 360K floppy disks on 1.2Mb drives.
/8	Formats with eight tracks instead of nine. This allows for compatibility with older versions of DOS (before version 2.0).
/DESTROY	Formats and overwrites data.
/F	Allows a full format. PC Format will read each track, format each track, and then rewrite the original data back to the disk. This is to correct marginal sector ID's.
/F:*nnn*	Formats the disk to a specific size. Values are as follows: 160, 180, 320, 360, 720, 1200, and 1440.
/N:*xx*	Specifies how many sectors per track to format. Must also specify the /T:*xx* parameter to indicate how many tracks to format.
/P	Prints the information to the printer. The information will go to LPT1.

Option	*Effect*
/Q	Performs a quick format on an already formatted disk. Only writes over the FAT and the directory. It does not scan the media's surface.
/R	Reformats and rewrites every track. Like the /F parameter, it is used to clean up marginal sector ID's.
/S	Copies the operating system to the disk to make it bootable.
/T:*xx*	Specifies the number of tracks to format.
/TEST	Simulates a format, but will not write anything to the disk.
/V	Allows user to define a volume label.
/?	Displays all available options.

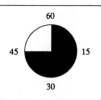

60
45   15
30

The Desktop program contains an editor more powerful than the PC Shell editor. Since Desktop allows up to fifteen windows to be open at one time, you can theoretically load fifteen different text files. In practice, however, you will probably not open more than two or three windows. Otherwise the screen would get rather cluttered.

In this step, you will learn how to create and edit text with the editor. Then, you will see the various alternatives for formatting and editing text blocks.

Creating a Text File

To create a new document or edit an existing file, select the Notepads function in the Desktop menu. A file selection window will be displayed. To create the text file in the directory currently being displayed, simply enter a file name and the .TXT file extension.

To store the text in a different directory, specify the drive identifier and the directory path. For example, to create a text file in the subdirectory named \TEXTS of the directory \PCTOOLS on drive C, proceed as follows:

```
C:\PCTOOLS\TEXTS\EXAMPLE.TXT   <Return>
```

After you press the Return key, the program issues a message stating that it did not find the file. You now have the option of creating this file or aborting the process altogether. Confirm creation of the new file with the Return key. The program provides an editor window for you to enter the text. Figure 14.1 shows this window with text already entered.

Contents

*Creating
a file*

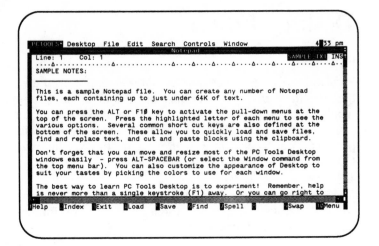

Figure 14.1: The Editor window

Opening a Second Window

Several windows

To create a second text file, restart the Notepads function in the Desktop menu. Proceed as described above to create a second file. Change the active window by pressing F9. This will swap the active window with the underlying window. If you have a mouse, simply click on an exposed portion of the underlying window.

Loading a File

To load an existing file, select this file in the file selection window and press the Return key. If an editor window is already open, press F4 to bring up the file selection window.

Storing a File

Saving a file

To store a file, press F5 or choose the Save function in the File menu, and the window displayed in Figure 14.2 will appear.

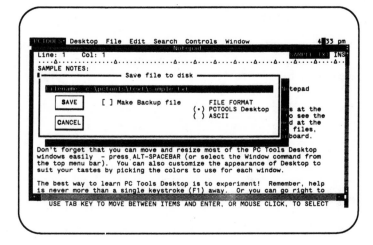

Figure 14.2: Saving a file

Specify how the file is to be saved in the dialog box that follows. Select the desired options from those available with the Tab key. You can specify whether a backup copy of the file is to be created with the file extension .BAK. You can also choose the format to be used to store the file. You have two choices in selecting an appropriate format for saving text:

| PC TOOLS DESKTOP | The program stores the file in Desktop format. The file retains all formatting commands. |
| ASCII | The program stores the file as a text file without any formatting information. |

Select the desired save mode with the cursor keys and confirm the choice with the Return key.

Editor Commands

You have several editor commands available for moving the cursor within text. The most important commands are covered in the following table:

Key	Effect
Cursor keys	Move the cursor one position in the corresponding direction.
Return	Begins a new paragraph.
Del	Deletes one character at the cursor.
Backspace	Erases one character to the left of the cursor.
Home	Moves the cursor to the beginning of the line.
End	Moves the cursor to the end of the line.
Ctrl-Home	Moves the cursor to the beginning of the file.
Ctrl-End	Moves the cursor to the end of the file.
Home-Home	Moves the cursor to the beginning of the window.
End-End	Moves the cursor to the end of the window.
PgUp	Scrolls up one window.
PgDn	Scrolls down one window.

To move the cursor to a specific line, select the Goto function in the Edit menu and enter the appropriate line number.

Marking a Text Block

Block editing

A text block must first be marked before moving or copying. You can mark a block with either the mouse or the keyboard.

To use the keyboard, first move the cursor to the start of the block. Select Mark block from the Edit menu. Now move the cursor to the end of the block with the cursor keys. The block is now marked. To use the mouse, move the mouse pointer to the beginning of the block, press the mouse button and drag the mouse pointer to the end of the block. To cancel the block mark, select the Unmark block function.

Moving a Marked Block

Move a previously marked block using the Cut to Clipboard function that is also found in the Edit menu. After starting the function, move the cursor to the point where you want to move the text. Then select the Paste from Clipboard function. The program deletes the text from its original position and inserts it at the desired point.

Moving a block

Copying a Marked Block

You can copy a marked block to another point in a similar manner. Select the Copy to Clipboard function and move the cursor to the point where the text is to be copied. Then use the Paste from Clipboard function to copy the text block. Text blocks can be copied from one window to another.

Copying a block

Finding and Replacing Text

The Search menu provides two functions for finding text characters and words. If you only wish to search for a term, select the Find function and enter the desired character string.

Find and replace

You can also replace the character string with the Replace function. A simpler method of calling this function is to press the F6 key. You will see the window displayed in Figure 14.3.

Enter the search term and the replace term and select among the available options with the Tab and Return keys. The

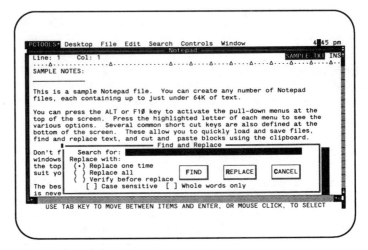

Figure 14.3: Searching and replacing character strings

following choices are available for finding and replacing terms with the Desktop editor.

Replace one time	The program only replaces the search term at the first position found.
Replace all	The program replaces the search term everywhere.
Verify before replace	You must confirm each replace operation.
Case sensitive	The program differentiates between uppercase and lowercase letters.
Whole words only	The program includes only complete words in the search. If you switch this option off with the Return key, you will also find the character string embedded within words.

Automatic Text Saving

In addition to the normal function for saving a text file, an automatic text-saving facility is available. It will save the text at previously specified intervals.

You should use this function in case of a power outage or power surge. It can save you a lot of time in not having to re-type the document over again. Select the Autosave function in the File menu and enter the interval in minutes between save operations. Then, press the Tab key and switch on the save mode with the Return key. Return to edit mode with the Alt-O key combination.

Autosave

Deleting Window Contents

The Delete all text function deletes the entire text but not the file containing the text. To delete the whole file use the Delete option in the file selection window.

Deleting

Inserting a File

To insert one text file into another text file, select the Insert file function in the Edit menu. From a file selection window, select the file that is to be inserted into the text. First move the cursor to the position where the text is to appear, then load it into the text with the Return key.

Inserting

Spell Checking

The editor has a spelling checker. Start the function either by pressing F7 or by selecting Spellcheck File from the Edit menu. You can select among three spell checking functions:

Spellcheck Word   The program checks only one word.

Spellcheck Screen   The program checks the section of
                       text displayed on the screen.

Spellcheck file   The program checks the entire text file.

If the program does not find a word, you may select from among four choices:

Ignore   Ignore the word and continue.

Correct   Correct the word by selecting from a list of suggested spellings or typing in a new spelling of your own.

Add   Add the word to the dictionary.

Quit   Abort spellchecking.

Select the desired function with the Tab key and start the function with the Return key.

Printing a Text File

Printing

Before printing a text file, specify the printer port and the page format.

Specifying the Output Device and Starting Printing

Specifying the printer

Select the Print function in the File menu and specify the printer port. The default is the LPT1 printer port. To use a different port, select that port with the cursor keys and confirm the choice with the Return key. Once the selection is made, start printing the text file with the Print function.

Page Format

Layout

Select the Page layout function in the Controls menu to specify the page format (see Figure 14.4).

You can specify the following format characteristics:

Left margin
Right margin

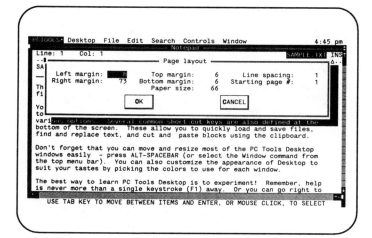

Figure 14.4: Page formatting

Top margin
Bottom margin
Paper size (in lines per page)
Line spacing
Starting page

The program retains all formatting characteristics only if you save the text file using the Desktop format. All format information will be lost in ASCII format.

Entering a Header and a Footer

The Header/Footer function allows entry of one header and one footer. These may be up to 50 characters long. To number the page, enter the # character where you want the pagination to appear.

Headers and footers

Configuring the Editor Window

Changing the window

In addition to window size, position, and color, other settings are available to configure the editor window. You must save all these settings later with the Save setup function on the Controls menu. The settings will then be available when you call the program again. You will not need to reset them each time.

You can find the following functions for configuration in the Controls menu:

Tab ruler edit	Specify the distance between tab stops here. Call the function and enter a number between 3 and 29. The default for this interval is 5 characters. After selecting the interval, press the Esc key and return to edit mode.
Tab ruler display ON	Toggle the display of the line ruler on or off with this function.
Overtype mode	This function switches overtype mode on or off and corresponds to the Ins key.
Control char display	The program displays all control characters.
Wordwrap on	The program starts automatic wordwrap; text adapts to the window size.
Auto indent	Each new line starts at the same position as the previous line.
Save setup	This stores all settings.

A check mark character preceding the name of the function indicates that the function is enabled.

Step 15

Outlines

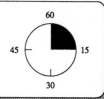

Desktop also contains a program for designing outlines. With this program, you can assemble ideas, rework thoughts or collect and hierarchically sort key words. The program functions are almost identical to those of the Notepad described in the previous step; there are only a few new commands. One difference is that the Outliner's program has no word wrap feature, but for outlining purposes this should pose no problems.

This step will show how to design and modify an outline with Desktop.

Creating an Outline File

Start the Outlines function in the Desktop menu and specify the name of the new file in the file selection window. Give the file an .OUT extension. You will then be able to find it when loading the selection list again, without having to change the file selection conditions. After you specify the name and press the Return key, the program issues a message that it can't find the specified file and that it will create a new file. Press the Return key to confirm; an outline window will appear. Design the outline in this window.

Editing Commands

The editing commands are identical to those in the previous step. Use the same keyboard commands for cursor movement. The Tab key alone has a different use when designing outlines.

The Tab key creates new outline levels corresponding to the hierarchical structure. To change the length of the tab stop, select the Tab ruler Edit function in the Controls menu and enter a number from 3 to 29. Exit this function with the Esc key.

Designing an Outline

Design

To design an outline, proceed as follows:

1. Enter the first outline item and finish with the Return key.

2. If another item is to be subordinate to this item, move the cursor to the end of the line above and press the Return key. Now press the Tab key, enter the subordinate item, and then finish with the Return key.

3. To enter another item at a level that is yet more subordinate, create the level following the step above. This level is subordinate to the first two levels. Move to the next higher level with the Tab key.

Outline Functions

All functions used to design an outline are found in the Headlines menu, shown in Figure 15.1. You can change, hide or highlight levels with these functions.

Hiding Levels

There are three choices for hiding subordinate levels. To hide all levels except the main items of the outline, select the Main headline only function. All subordinate items then disappear and only an arrowhead character (▶) indicates the existence of these levels (see Figure 15.2).

If you only want to hide the sublevels of one main outline item, move the cursor to the desired item and call the Collapse Current function.

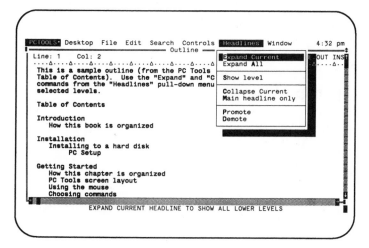

```
 PCTOOLS  Desktop  File  Edit  Search  Controls  Headlines  Window       4:32 pm
 ─────────────────────────────── Outline ───────
 Line: 1     Col: 2                          Expand Current          OUT INS
 ····∆····∆····∆····∆····∆····∆····∆····∆    Expand All           ·∆····∆··
 This is a sample outline (from the PC Tools
 Table of Contents).  Use the "Expand" and "C   Show level
 commands from the "Headlines" pull-down menu
 selected levels.                            Collapse Current
                                             Main headline only
 Table of Contents
                                             Promote
 Introduction                                Demote
    How this book is organized

 Installation
    Installing to a hard disk
         PC Setup

 Getting Started
    How this chapter is organized
    PC Tools screen layout
    Using the mouse
    Choosing commands

 ─────────── EXPAND CURRENT HEADLINE TO SHOW ALL LOWER LEVELS ───────────
```

Figure 15.1: Displaying different levels

To reduce the entire display to specific levels, use the Show level function. For example, if the outline has four levels and you only wish to display two of these, move the cursor to any heading item on the second level and select Show level.

Displaying Hidden Levels

There are two ways to display hidden levels. If you just want to display the subordinate levels of one main outline item, move the cursor to this item and select the Expand Current function. To display all hidden levels, select the Expand All function. The program then displays all levels.

Changing Levels

The Promote and Demote functions permit changing the hierarchical arrangement of individual outline items. Move the cursor to the appropriate item and select the Promote function to move this item one level higher. The program also copies all subordinate items to the next higher level.

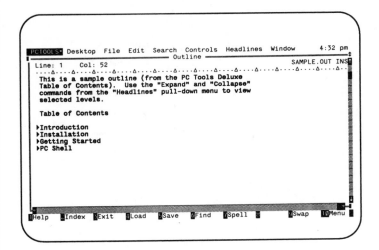

Figure 15.2: Main headline only display

The Demote function operates in an opposite manner. After you have moved the cursor to the outline item and called the function, the program moves this item to the next lower level.

Storing an Outline

Saving the file

Storing an outline is performed just as in the Desktop Notepads editor. You have the choice of storing the outline file in Desktop format or as an ASCII file. To continue editing the outline using another program, select ASCII format. The Desktop format, while maintaining the color setting of the outline window, cannot be used by other programs.

Step 16

Database

Desktop also provides a database program that can even be used to generate form letters. With a Hayes-compatible modem, you can also dial telephone numbers directly from the database.

This step will show how to define a file, enter records, and conduct searches according to different criteria. Once the file is created, you will learn how to produce form letters with format files.

Creating a New File

Call the Databases program in the Desktop menu and enter the name of the new file in the file selection window. Give this file a .DBF extension. This file can be used later by dBASE III or IV. After entering the name, press the Return key or Alt-N and specify the structure of the file in the field editor. Proceed as follows:

1. Enter the name of the field and press the Return key.

2. Specify the field type (see Figure 16.1). The following choices are available:

    Character   Designates a character string that may contain up to 70 characters.

    Numeric   Stands for a numeric field that may contain 19 digits.

    Logical   Designates a logical field that recognizes only the difference between True (represented by T, t, Y, or y) and False (designated by F, f, N, or n). A logical field contains only one character.

Date   Stands for a date field containing eight characters. The form is MM/DD/YY.

Only the field type definition is needed if you wish to import data from dBASE or export data to dBASE.

If you will be using the database file primarily in Desktop, define only Character type fields, because you can also enter numbers in these fields. The other options are provided to make exporting to dBASE more logical.

Saving the file

Next, specify the size of the field and, if you have selected a numeric field, the number of digits to the right of the decimal point. Once you have finished the field definition, use the Add command to add the field to the file. Specify all necessary fields one after another in this way. Once the field definition is finished, use the Save command to store the file.

Changing the file structure

You can page through the fields with the Next and Prev commands to make changes in the structure. To edit, choose the

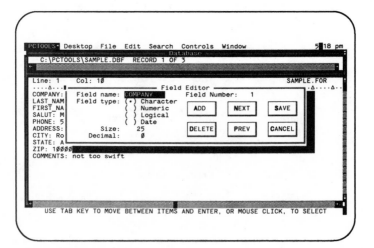

Figure 16.1: Field definition

Edit Fields command in the Edit menu. However, be careful. Editing can cause you to lose data. For example, if you choose to add a new field, the program will in essence create a new database. The old data will be lost, so make a backup copy of your database. You can always append or transfer this information into the updated database at a later time. The following edit command options are supported:

Add   Adds a new field definition to the database.
Next   Moves to the next field name.
Save   Saves changes and closes the dialog box.
Delete   Deletes a field.
Previous   Moves back to the previous field name.
Cancel   Closes the dialog box.

Entering Data Records

Once you have finished and saved the field definition, you can work with the file in the Database window, as shown in Figure 16.2.

*Entering
data*

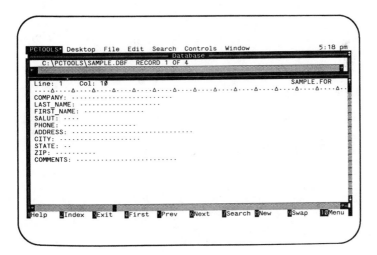

Figure 16.2: The Database window

Press F8 or select the Add new records function in the Edit menu. Enter a new data record. You must call this function again every time you wish to add a new record.

Paging Through the Data Records

After you have entered the first records, the following function keys allow paging through the file:

Key	Effect
F4	Moves to the beginning of the file or the end of the file.
F5	Moves back one record.
F6	Moves forward one record.

Editing a Data Record

Changing data records

Data records can be changed at any time. Select the desired record, move the cursor to the desired field, and overwrite the contents. The program is in overtype mode, so if you want to change it, press the Ins key. The program automatically stores the new contents when you press the Return key.

Deleting a Data Record

Deleting data records

Select the record to be deleted and call the Delete records function in the Edit menu. The program marks the record for deletion and no longer displays it. To cancel the deletion, select the Undelete records function.

The program keeps all records marked for deletion available. If you wish to completely remove these records from the file, use the Pack database function.

Hiding Data Records

You may hide the current data record with the Hide current record function. Although the file still contains the record, the program will no longer display it. You can hide all data records except one. The Select all records function makes the hidden data records visible again.

Editing Field Names

The Edit fields function in the Edit menu allows changing the field names and their structure.

Sorting a File

Files can be sorted according to any record. Proceed by calling the Sort database function in the Edit menu. Select the field to be used with the Next and Prev commands (see Figure 16.3). These are used to page through the fields.

Sorting data records

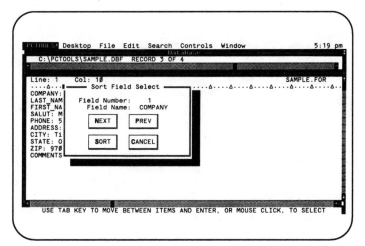

Figure 16.3: Sorting the file according to a data field

Using the Tab key, select the Sort command and start it with
the Return key. The file is then appropriately sorted according
to the chosen field.

Selecting Data Records

*Selecting
data
records*

Select data records with the Select records function found in
the Edit menu. Enter the name of the field to be used as the
selection criterion in the left column of the record selection
window. Enter the corresponding selection term in the right
column (see Figure 16.4).

Up to eight different fields and selection criteria can be combined for record selection. You can specify letters or numbers, ranges of letters or numbers, or wildcard characters.
When all the conditions for selection have been met, all other
records will be hidden.

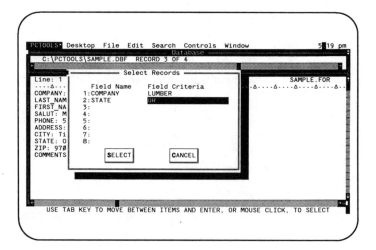

Figure 16.4: Selecting data records

Searching Data Records

The Search menu offers three choices for searching data records. The Goto record function displays a particular record after you have entered the record number. In normal use, this function is not very practical (unless you know about where in the database the record is stored) and most people will seldom employ it. The two other search methods allow searching for data records by entry of an appropriate search condition.

Select the Find text in Sort field option, if you wish to search for a record according to the contents of the sort field. This method is very fast because the program finds the sorting characteristics in an additional field bearing the same name and differing only by the .REC file extension. Thus it looks only in the field used for sorting.

If you wish to enter any search term, select the Find text in all fields function.

This method searches all fields of a record and takes more time. In both methods, you first enter the search term. Then you select whether the program is to search for the term only in selected records, from the current record forward or in the entire file (see Figure 16.5). Start the search with the Alt-S key combination.

Printing a File

Decide which data records are to be printed with the Print function on the File menu. You may select from three different print modes:

Print selected records   The program prints only the records selected previously.

Searching

Printing

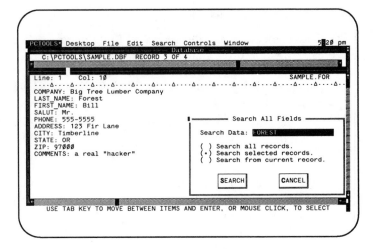

```
PCTOOLS▾ Desktop  File  Edit  Search  Controls  Window        5 20 pm
                              Database
     C:\PCTOOLS\SAMPLE.DBF   RECORD 3 OF 4

  Line: 1    Col: 10                                     SAMPLE.FOR
  ····Δ····Δ····Δ····Δ····Δ····Δ····Δ····Δ····Δ····Δ····Δ····Δ··
  COMPANY: Big Tree Lumber Company
  LAST_NAME: Forest
  FIRST_NAME: Bill
  SALUT: Mr.
  PHONE: 555-5555                      ┌──── Search All Fields ────┐
  ADDRESS: 123 Fir Lane                │
  CITY: Timberline                     │ Search Data: FOREST
  STATE: OR                            │
  ZIP: 97000                           │ ( ) Search all records.
  COMMENTS: a real "hacker"            │ (•) Search selected records.
                                       │ ( ) Search from current record.
                                       │
                                       │  ┌────────┐   ┌────────┐
                                       │  │ SEARCH │   │ CANCEL │
                                       │  └────────┘   └────────┘

     USE TAB KEY TO MOVE BETWEEN ITEMS AND ENTER, OR MOUSE CLICK, TO SELECT
```

Figure 16.5: Entering the search term

Print current record	The program prints only the current record.
Print field names	The program prints only the field names of the file. Select this option if you need the field names to generate a form letter and do not have the names available elsewhere.

Next, press Alt-P and specify the printer port. Press Alt-P again to start printing.

Writing a Form Letter

Form letters

You can also design simple form letters in combination with the editor. Every database file creates a format file having the .FOR file extension. You can manually generate any number of format files for each database file (see Figure 16.6). For

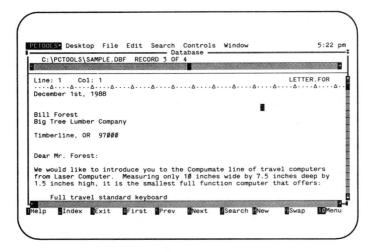

Figure 16.6: Creating a format file

example, you can define different print formats to print letters and address labels using a single address file. It is a good idea to use the form files supplied with PC Tools as models in creating your own. To write a form letter, proceed as follows:

1. In Desktop, call the Notepads editor, create a file with a .FOR extension, and enter the text. Enter the appropriate field names in square brackets where field contents of the database are to appear.

2. Call the database program if it is not already loaded in a window and select the file for which you have created the format file.

3. Select the Load form function in the File menu. The program now shows the records of the file with the newly defined format.

4. Select the desired data records.

5. Define the page format in the Controls menu. See Step 14 for more information on page format features.

6. Call the Print function from the File menu and start printing.

This way, you can generate not only form letters but also any other type of formatted printing. Other choices could be the printing of labels or index cards. Multipage printing is also possible.

Dialing Telephone Numbers

Modem functions

With a Hayes-compatible modem, you may also dial telephone numbers automatically from the database program. To use this function, remember to specify the field containing the telephone numbers as the first field when defining the structure of the file. While the program does search in all fields, it does not distinguish between different fields containing numbers. If, for example, you had a field containing the Zip code before the telephone-number field, the program would interpret the Zip code as a dialable number.

Generating the configuration

Before using this function, you must call the Configure Autodial function in the Controls menu and specify the transfer parameters (see Figure 16.7). You must specify the following:

Parameters

1. Dialing method

For a push-button telephone, select the Tone dial option. Otherwise, select the Pulse dial function.

2. Port

Specify the serial port to which the modem is connected.

3. Baud Rate

Select the baud rate.

4. Access Code

Select the access code to get an outside line.

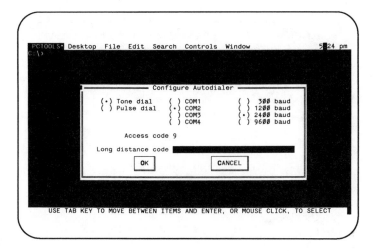

Figure 16.7: Setting the transmission parameters

5. Long Distance Code   Enter 1 for long distance. If
                         you have not placed the area
                         code in the database, then you
                         can do it here.

Note: The Access code and Long Distance Code are global
for all numbers dialed in the database, however the program does give you the chance to override this before it tries
to dial.

Select the individual options with the cursor keys and confirm them with the Return key.

After providing all the configuration information, select the
Save setup function to save the settings.

Saving the settings

To dial a telephone number, proceed as follows:

1. Specify the data record containing the number to be
   dialed.

2. Call the Autodial function in the Controls menu. After the program has dialed the number, pick up the receiver and use the Disconnect modem function or press the ESC key before the other party answers.

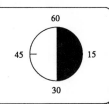

Step 17

Appointment Scheduler

The appointment scheduler found in Desktop allows you to plan your time effectively. In order to make full use of the scheduler, you must install Desktop in memory-resident mode. The alarm function that reminds you of upcoming appointments operates only in this mode. This step will show how to create a schedule file and how to take care of all appointment scheduling using this file. You will also see the different facilities for configuring the appointment scheduler to your wishes.

Creating a Schedule File

Enter the file name and path in the file selection window to create the schedule file. After confirming the request asking whether you wish to create a new file, the new file becomes available. If several people use the same computer, each person should create his or her own file.

Loading the Schedule File

To load a different file into the Appointment scheduler, select the Load function in the File window. Choose the file containing your appointments with the cursor keys. Start this file with the Alt-L key combination. The Appointment scheduler is shown in Figure 17.1.

Saving a Schedule File

After you have finished scheduling appointments, save the file with the Save function in the File menu. To have the program save the file automatically at specified intervals, use the Autosave function. As in the other Desktop program sections, it is recommended that you specify an interval for automatic saving.

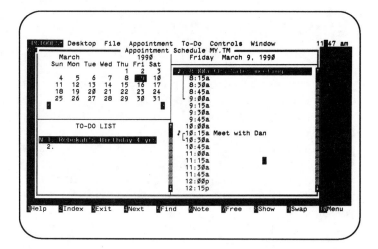

Figure 17.1: Appointment scheduler

Entering Appointments

Once you have created your personal schedule file, there are several choices you may make. In addition to the monthly calendar field, there is the Appointment Schedule window, and the To-Do list window. Press the Tab key to select between the three available windows. You may also create a priority To-Do list. Enter the things you have to do and specify their order of importance.

To enter an appointment, proceed as follows:

1. Select the monthly calendar field with the Tab key. Using the cursor keys, specify the day for which you wish to make entries.

2. Switch to the appointment field with the Tab key. Select the time at which the appointment begins with the cursor keys.

3. Enter a heading and press the Return key. You will see the window displayed in Figure 17.2.

4. Specify all the important details of the appointment to be entered in the window. The following items can be specified:

Start date   Contains the selected date.

End date   Specify here the last day on which the appointment is valid. The default is no end date.

Time   Displays the selected time. You can still change both the date and the starting time.

Note   Allows you to enter a brief note or attach a macro to an appointment.

Type   Here you may classify appointments to find them more easily later. The type is limited to one character.

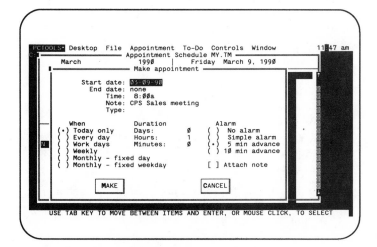

Figure 17.2: Entering an appointment

When	Specify here the day of the week and the month on which the appointment is valid.
Duration	Select the duration of the appointment.
Alarm	Decide whether to start the alarm function. This option only works effectively in memory-resident mode.
Attach Note	You may attach a note to your appointment with this option.

5. Then, select the Make command and confirm it with the Return key. The appointments list now contains the newly entered appointment. A solid line displays the duration of the appointment.

Switch between the individual options with the Tab key. Use the Return key to start the appropriate option.

Creating a To-Do List

If you wish only to make entries that are not tied to specific times, enter these in the To-Do list window.

Proceed as follows:

1. Select the To-Do list window with the Tab key. Enter the title and confirm with Return.

2. Now enter the start and end dates in the New to-do entry window (see Figure 17.3). Specify the importance in the Priority field. This information will control the later display in the schedule file.

3. Decide whether to create a note with the Attach note option. Then choose the Make command to create the entry.

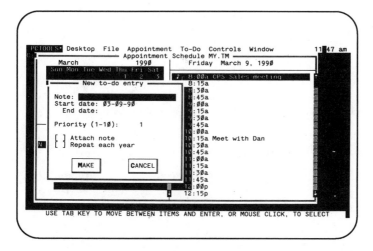

Figure 17.3: Creating a priority list

To delete an entry, specify it with the cursor keys. Then call the Delete to-do entry function in the To-Do menu.

Deleting the Entry

Configuring the Schedule File

The Controls menu provides various facilities for configuring the file to your special taste.

Configuration

Call the Appointment settings function. Specify the screen display of the schedule file.

You may change the following components (see Figure 17.4):

Work days	Specify the work days of the week.
Start time	Specify the beginning of the day for your appointment scheduler.
Stop time	Specify the end of your work day.

Increment   Decide whether the display will use fif-
               teen-minute or thirty-minute intervals.

Date format   Specify the date format.

Time format   Specify the format for the time of day.

Then confirm the configuration with the OK command.

Specifying Holidays

The Holiday settings function in the Controls menu allows
you to enter movable and fixed holidays. This is a great place
to specify birthdays and anniversaries.

Editing Appointments

To edit an appointment, select it with the cursor keys and call
the Edit appointment function in the Appointment menu. You

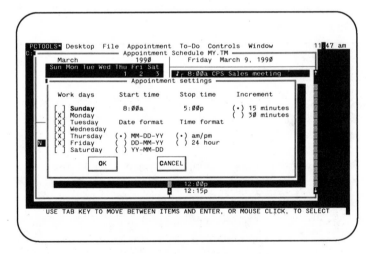

Figure 17.4: Configuring Appointment settings

have the same options in the editing window as you did for entering an appointment.

Deleting an Appointment

To delete an appointment, select it with the cursor keys and call the Delete appointment function. The program deletes the appointment from the list.

Adding Notes

You can add notes later to both appointments and items on the To-Do list. Select the entry to which you wish to add the note and press F6.

The program automatically creates a file for the selected entry. This file may be edited with the Desktop Notepads editor. Press F6 again to view the note later.

Determining Free Time

To determine the remaining free time, call the Find free time function in the Appointment menu.

Select whether you wish to check only work days or also holidays and enter the desired time duration. The function will check up to the next 365 days to find the required length of time.

Displaying the Week's Assignments

The Show time usage function, also found in the Appointment menu, gives a graphical display of free and scheduled time for five days (see Figure 17.5).

Schedule for the week

This function always displays the next five days including the day selected in the calendar window.

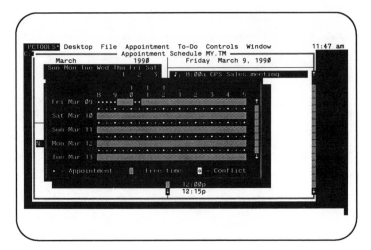

Figure 17.5: Displaying the week assignment

Printing the Appointment List

Printing

To print a list of your entered appointments, call the Print function in the File menu. Specify whether you want to print only a daily list, a weekly list or a monthly list. The Translate graphic characters option allows conversion of the graphics characters used in the screen display. Since many printers cannot create these characters, the function replaces them with other characters.

Calling Macros

Macros

The appointment scheduler also allows you to automatically call macros created with the Macro Editor (see Step 20). When entering a new appointment, enter the pipe symbol ¦ in the Note field followed by the key combination used to start the macro. If, for example, you wish to start a telecommunications program at a specific time, make the following entry:

```
Telecommunications¦ <CtrlF10>
```

This entry calls a macro started with Ctrl-F10 at a specific time. This way, you may start any program using macros in the appointment scheduler. The PC Tools Deluxe manual provides a wide assortment of powerful macros with the appointment scheduler.

Step 18

Calculators

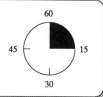

There are four different calculators available in Desktop. Besides a simple calculator for algebraic functions, there is an HP-16C compatible programmer's calculator, an HP-12C compatible financial calculator, and an HP-11C compatible scientific calculator.

This step will introduce the basic operations of all four calculators. It will only touch upon HP-compatible calculators because of their complexity. However, there are other publications that walk the user through the complexities of these calculators.

Algebraic Calculator

To use the algebraic calculator for simple computations, call the Algebraic calculator function in the Calculators menu (see Figure 18.1).

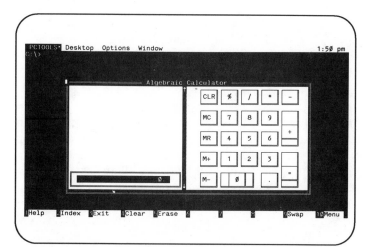

Figure 18.1: Algebraic calculator

The calculator layout is very Spartan. However, the operation is designed to be so easy that you do not need additional information.

Simply enter the first number, then the operator, and then the second number. To perform the calculation, press the Return key. You can also perform more extensive computations in the same way.

The following operators are available:

Operators

Operator/Key	Effect
+	Addition
−	Subtraction
*	Multiplication
/	Division
Return	Result
C	Clear the display
%	Calculate a percentage
M, then +	Add the number to the memory
M, then −	Subtract the number from the memory
M + R	Fetch the number from the memory
M + C	Clear the number from memory
D and a number	Specify the number of decimal places

Editing the Paper Tape

"Paper Tape"

To see the results of previous computations again, scroll through the paper tape with the cursor keys or the PgUp and PgDn keys. The paper tape retains all previous calculator operations and the results. To "tear off" the simulated paper tape, press the F5 key. The tape disappears and the previous results are cleared.

Copying Calculations to the Clipboard

To copy the calculations and results to the editor or outline program, select the Copy to Clipboard function in the Options Menu. The program copies all operands shown in the calculator and the result automatically to the Clipboard. Then call the editor or the outline program and move the cursor to that point where you wish to insert the computation. Select the Paste from Clipboard function in the Edit menu. This function copies the contents from the Clipboard.

Copying results

Financial and Scientific Calculators

This section will only mention the financial and scientific calculators briefly, because the scope of their operations would fill several volumes. The financial calculator is shown in Figure 18.2.

You may want to purchase the additional books recommended in the PC Tools Desktop manual. They will help greatly in using the calculator options.

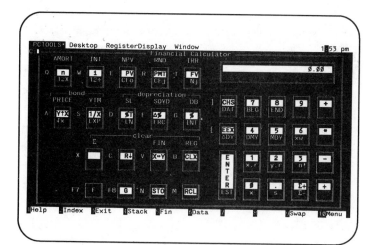

Figure 18.2: Financial calculator

A simple calculation will explain the input mode. For example, to calculate (123 + 234) * 12, proceed as follows:

1. Enter 123 and press the Return key.
2. Enter 234 and press the + key.
3. Enter 12 and press the * key.

Remember that the program does not read all keyboards the same way. With expanded multifunction keyboards, you may have to select some operators in the cursor block and some using the standard keyboard. An example of this is the / key.

HP-16C Programmer's Calculator

The primary use of the HP-16C programmer's calculator (see Figure 18.3) is programming work. The programmer's calculator does computations in four different number systems: decimal, binary, octal, and hexadecimal. Using the cursor

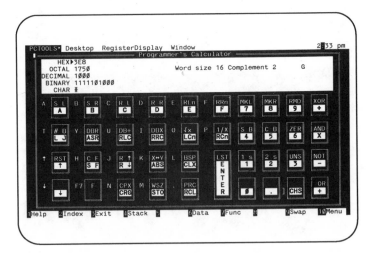

Figure 18.3: The HP-16C Programmer's calculator

keys, select the number system and proceed as with the algebraic calculator. The calculator then displays the results in all four number systems.

As with the other HP compatible calculators, if you are not familiar with the programmer's calculator, it is recommended you read additional instructional material besides that provided by Central Point Software in the manuals.

Telecommunications

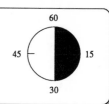

Desktop also contains a telecommunications program. While this program is not the equal of dedicated telecommunications programs, it is adequate for simple purposes. It will let you communicate with virtually any other computer system via a modem. It can also send faxes, if you have a fax board installed on your computer or somewhere in your network.

In this step you will learn how to create a phone directory file and to dial computers using a Hayes-compatible modem. You can also use this program for simple file transfers between two computers as well as for sending a fax.

Loading the Phone Directory File

To call the telecommunications program, select the Telecommunications program in the Desktop menu. A second pop-up menu appears to give you choices between modem telecommunications, sending a fax, or checking the fax log. Choose Modem Telecommunications. When the program starts, it automatically loads the existing phone directory file (see Figure 19.1).

Loading a file

Creating a Phone Directory File

To create one or more of your own files, select the Load function in the File menu. Enter the name of the new file in the file window. Give the file a .TEL extension so that this file will appear later in the file selection window. After you have confirmed creation of the file, this file appears on the screen. In order to make an entry, select the Create new entry function in the Edit menu (see Figure 19.2). Enter the following parameters needed for transmission:

Creating a file

    NAME   Enter the name of the recipient or the mailbox.

Parameters

PHONE	Enter the telephone number.
SCRIPT	Specify the name of a command file for automating the transmission (optional).
USER ID	Enter a user ID (normally used when logging onto a bulletin board service).
PASSWORD	Enter a confidential password (used primarily on bulletin boards).
DATABASE	Enter the path and file name of a database that contains fields of data you would like to send, such as a phone number or fax number (optional).
FIELD1/FIELD2	Enter two fields in the database that contain data to be sent (optional).
TERMINAL	Select the desired terminal emulation.

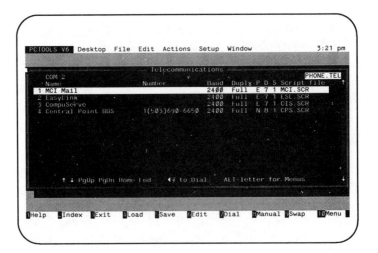

Figure 19.1: Telecommunications window

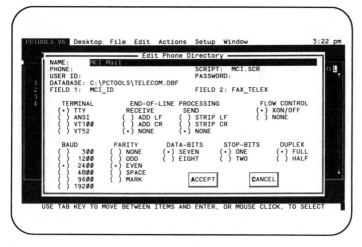

Figure 19.2: Entering telecommunications parameters

END-OF-LINE	Specify the characters used to mark the end of a line.

Receive:

ADD LF	Adds a line feed for incoming data.
ADD CR	Adds a carriage return for incoming data.
NONE	Adds no line feed or carriage return.

Send:

STRIP LF	Removes line feed.
STRIP CR	Removes carriage return.
NONE	No strip; the Return key sends the carriage return.

FLOW CONTROL	Controls the flow of data between two computers, to help decrease chance of lost data.
XON/XOFF	Buffers the data flow between the computers.
NONE	The data is buffered, but to a lesser degree. There is a greater chance of lost data.
BAUD	Specifies the rate of data transmission. The rate must match the computer you are connected with.
PDS	Specifies the way data will be sent. Both systems must be set up the same.
PARITY	An error detecting bit.
DATA BITS	Specifies the number of bits in a transmitted character.
STOP BIT	Used to indicate the end of a character.
DUPLEX	Select half-duplex or full-duplex transmission.

Editing the Entry

Changing the entry

Position the cursor bar on the entry to be changed and select the Edit entry function in the Edit menu. You may redefine all telecommunications parameters in the following editing menu.

Deleting an Entry

Deleting an entry

To delete an entry, you must mark the entry with the cursor bar. Then call the Remove entry function in the Edit menu.

Saving the File

As in the other Desktop programs, select the Save function in the File menu to save your file.

Configuring the Modem

Select the Modem setup function in the Setup menu. Enter the appropriate information.

Setting the modem

COM PORT	Select the serial port connected to your modem.
DIALING	Specify what type of phone; pulse or tone.
MODEM INIT STRING	Specify which initialization string is needed for your modem.
CONNECT STRING	This string is sent by the modem to tell the telecommunications program that a connection was made.

Making a Connection

Two different methods are available for making a connection. With a Hayes-compatible modem, use the Dial function in the Actions menu. This automatically dials the number and makes the connection. If you only wish to exchange files between two computers via modem, start the Manual function.

Transferring Files

There are two different protocols available to transfer files. You should use the XMODEM protocol, because the ASCII protocol does not have error correction.

File transfer

Receiving Files

Receiving

To receive and store a file, choose a protocol from the Receive menu. After choosing either the ASCII or the XMODEM protocol, first enter the file name, then select Save. At the end of an ASCII transfer, call the End transfer function in the Actions menu. This function ends file transfer. When using the XMODEM protocol, the file transfer ends automatically.

Sending a File

Sending

Select the desired protocol in the Send menu. Then specify the file to be sent in the file selection window.

Next start the Load command that transfers the file (see Figure 19.3). If the XMODEM protocol is selected, you will receive a message telling whether the transfer has occurred without errors.

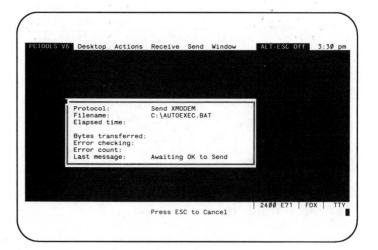

Figure 19.3: XMODEM protocol message

Background Communication

The telecommunications program also has a background mode. This means that you can transmit or receive files while working with a different program. To use this option, load the auxiliary Backtalk program and then load Desktop into memory in memory-resident mode. This program permits background communication. The serial port to be used for the background communication may be specified with the /N parameter. For example, if you want the transfer to use the COM 2 port, start Backtalk like this:

```
BACKTALK /2 <Return>
```

Remember that you may not run a program in the foreground that addresses the port used to transfer files in the background.

During background transfer of files, a blinking "B" in the top right corner of the screen indicates that the program is currently receiving or sending a file.

In addition, when operating in background mode, the program creates a file named TRANSFER.LOG. This file contains all messages about successful or unsuccessful transmissions.

Once a transmission is completed, the program beeps three times to announce the end of transmission.

Control Files

The telecommunications program also offers a small programming language for creating script files. Only a brief mention of this facility will be given here. You will find a complete overview of the commands and a few example files in the PC Tools Deluxe manual. Use the Desktop editor to generate such files. These files can be used to automate logging onto bulletin boards.

Command language

Commands

RECEIVE	Receive a variable.
SEND	Send a variable or character string.
WAITFOR	Wait for a character string.
PRINT	Display a variable or character string on the screen.
DOWNLOAD	Specify additional protocol names and file names to receive a file.
UPLOAD	Specify protocol names and file names here to send a file.

A small sample program to log onto a computer bulletin board, where the user ID is 240661 and the password is - - -.

```
"User id is 240661 and my password is- - -"
WAITFOR "User id?"
SEND "240661"
WAITFOR "password"
SEND "- - -"
PRINT "Here we go"
```

Configuring Fax Communications

Configur-ing the system for fax

1. Choose Telecommunications from the Desktop menu. When the pop-up menu appears, select Send Fax.

2. Choose the Fax Drive command from the Configure menu. Enter the directory name used by the Fax Tele-communications program. This was created when running PCSETUP.

3. Tab to the OK button and press the Return key.

Setting the Page Length

1. Select Page Length from the Configure menu and make your changes. The default setting is 11 inches.

2. Select the OK button.

Setting the Cover Page Option

1. Choose the Cover Page function from the Configure menu.

2. Specify a cover page if you wish to send one. The program will let you create one in a Notepads file.

3. Select OK.

Setting the Time Format

1. Choose the Time Format option from the Configure menu. Specify either 24 hour or AM/PM display.

2. Select OK.

Identifying the Sender

1. Select the Sent From option in the Configure menu.

2. Type in your name.

3. Select OK.

Sending a New Fax

1. Select Telecommunications from the Desktop menu. Choose Send a fax from the second pop-up menu.

2. Choose Add a new entry function from the Actions menu. You are presented with a screen of fax details.

*Sending
a fax*

The following is a list of the items you need to fill in:

Date	The program enters the current date, but you can modify this.
Time	The program enters the current time.
From	Specifies who the fax is from.
To	Specifies to whom the fax is sent.
Fax Number	The fax number of the destination.
Comments	You can identify your fax with the comments line. It is useful for identifying the fax in the future.
Normal Resolution	Select this option when sending letters.
Fine Resolution	Specify Fine resolution for graphics or pictures.
Fax board to Fax board	Select this option to send binary files.

3. To send an existing file choose the Select Files and Send option. This will bring up the Files to Select dialog box. Specify the file you want to send and select the Add function. This will add it to the Files to Send dialog box for future reference.

4. Choose Send from the Files to Send dialog box.

Once a fax has been sent, you can check on its status in the Fax log. To do this, choose the Telecommunications function in Desktop. When the second pop-up menu appears, select the Check fax log option.

Step 20

Clipboard/Macro Editor

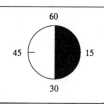

The Clipboard and Macro Editor programs are two practical utilities that you can use in many ways. With Clipboard, you copy sections of the screen from one program to another. For example, you can copy a section from a spreadsheet into your word processor. Use the Macro Editor to store and recall frequently used commands and keystrokes. You can use them to "play back" text strings. You can even start other programs using these macros. Another important use of macros is for printer control, because the Desktop editor cannot provide character formatting.

This last step shows how to copy sections from one program into another with Clipboard and shows what facilities are available to edit text. You will then learn how to create macros to automate program calls. Finally, this step covers the ASCII table. This table gives the decimal and hexadecimal value for any character.

Clipboard

While Clipboard has most of the important editing commands found with the Notepads editor, it is limited to a file size of 4K.This means that only about 80 lines of text can be copied to Clipboard at any given time. Clipboard must be memory-resident if it is to copy portions of screens from one application to another.

Copying a Section of the Screen

To copy a specific area from one program into another, proceed as follows:

1. Start Desktop and select the Clipboard program.

2. Call Copy to Clipboard in the Copy/Paste menu.

3. A block cursor is now available in the application pro-
    gram for marking text. Move the cursor to the begin-
    ning of the block and press the Return key. Mark the
    section of the screen and press the Return key again.
    The program copies the marked section into Clipboard.

4. Exit Desktop and start the program into which you
    want to copy the section.

5. Move the cursor to the insertion point and then start
    Desktop.

6. Call the Paste from Clipboard function in the Copy/
    Paste menu. The program now copies the section from
    the clipboard into the application program.

Editing Sections of the Screen

Editing

The editing commands of other Desktop programs are available in Clipboard with the Edit menu. You may mark and delete blocks of text (see Figure 20.1) move to lines of text and
even insert text files.

Simplifying Use by Hotkeys

Hotkeys

If you load Desktop as a stand-alone DOS application, you
must use the commands described above for copying sections of the screen. If you have loaded Desktop as memory-
resident, you can copy sections of the screen using hotkeys.
(If you are using an application other than Desktop, you must
load Desktop as memory-resident to use the clipboard.) Press
the Ctrl-Del key combination to copy a section into the clipboard and the Ctrl-Ins key combination to copy the section
into another program. If you wish to assign other hotkeys, use
the Utilities option in the Desktop menu. Choose the Hotkey
selection function and specify the desired key combination.

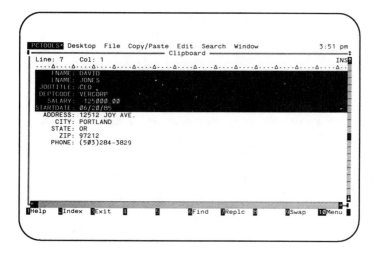

Figure 20.1: Marking a section of the screen

Macro Editor

With the Macro Editor, you can assign specific hotkeys to frequently used functions or programs. The program must be memory-resident if the hotkeys are to be effective outside Desktop.

Macros

Creating a Macro File

Start the Load function in the File menu and enter the name of the file. Remember to give the file a .PRO extension. The Macro Editor uses the familiar editing commands. To load an existing macro file, select the file with the cursor keys and press the Return key.

Creating a file

Writing a Macro

Macros have a simple syntax that does not present problems. Every macro begins with the expression *<begdef>* and ends

Creating a macro

with *<enddef>*. Remember these expressions must be enclosed in angle brackets. To write a macro that calls, for example, the algebraic calculator, proceed as follows:

1. Start the macro with the *<begdef>* expression.

2. Then press the key combination to start the macro. If you wish to use keys used by the Macro Editor, first press the F7 key. The program automatically encloses the key combination in parentheses.

3. Add the call *<desk>* in angle brackets to start Desktop.

4. Then enter the letter in bold or a different color used to call the calculator in Desktop.

5. End the macro with the *<enddef>* expression.

The finished macro looks like this:

```
<begdef><ctrlf4><desk>CA<enddef>
```

Start the calculator with the Ctrl-F4 key combination.

If, for example, you want to start PC Secure with the Ctrl-F8 key combination, write the following macro:

```
<begdef><ctrlf8>cd\pctools<enter>
pcsecure<enter><enddef>.
```

The Macro Editor is particularly well suited for controlling printers. You will find various macros for printer control in the PC Tools Deluxe manual.

Use the macros and replace the escape sequences with the commands corresponding to your printer if necessary.

For specific purposes, create files in which you define several macros.

Starting a Macro

Once you have finished creating the macro, select the Macro activation function in the File menu or press the F8 key. Specify where the macro should be active. The following choices are available:

Starting a macro

Not active	The macro is not active.
Active when in PC Tools Desktop	The macro is active only in Desktop.
Active when not in PC Tools Desktop	The macro only operates when you have not started Desktop (but have loaded it in memory-resident mode).
Active everywhere	The macro is available everywhere.

Select the desired choice and confirm it with the Return key.

ASCII Table

Desktop also has an ASCII table that displays the complete ASCII character set with hexadecimal and decimal values. If you are looking for the value of a specific key, press the key. The program then displays that key in the window. Scroll through the table with the cursor keys.

ASCII table

Index